D1233229

JAPANESE NOTEBOOKS

IGORT

JAPANESE NOTEBOOKS

A JOURNEY TO THE EMPIRE OF SIGNS

CHRONICLE BOOKS
SAN FRANCISCO

The Journey

I'd be lying if I said that it all began unexpectedly. Before I set foot there in spring 1991, I'd been dreaming of Japan for at least ten years. Since, in other words, I had started drawing it, almost unconsciously, for what would become my first book-length comic: "Goodbye Baobab."
"What was I looking for?" A question that has been with me for at least 25 years now.

After that, bit by bit, that mysterious place got under my skin.
Wanderlust and longing even led me to live there for a while in the '90s.
This book is the story of chasing a dream, and surrendering upon finding that dreams cannot be grasped.

塚治虫

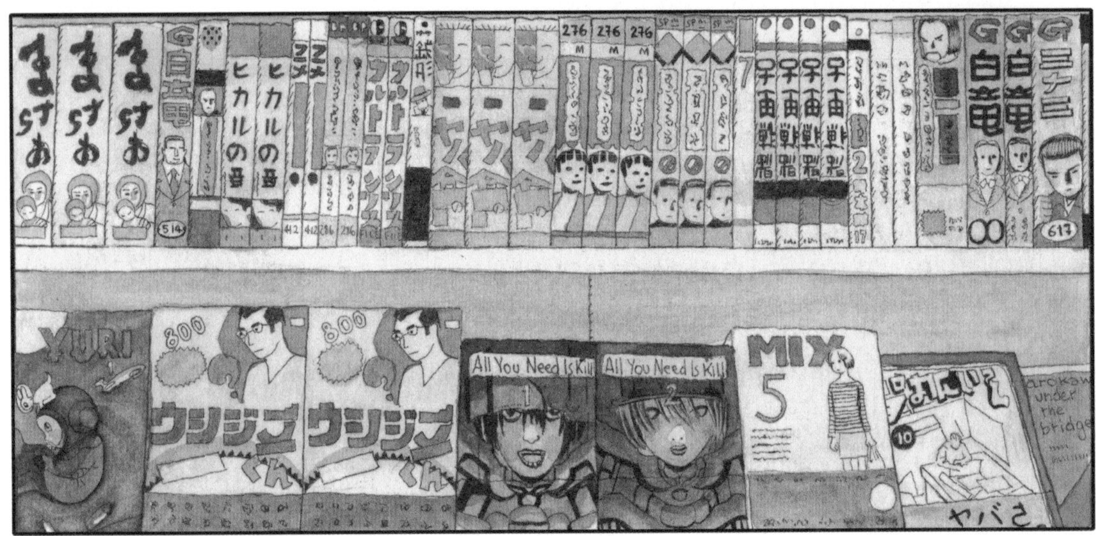
YURI
800
800
All You Need Is Kill
All You Need Is Kill
MIX
5
arakawa under the bridge
ヤバさ
白竜
白竜

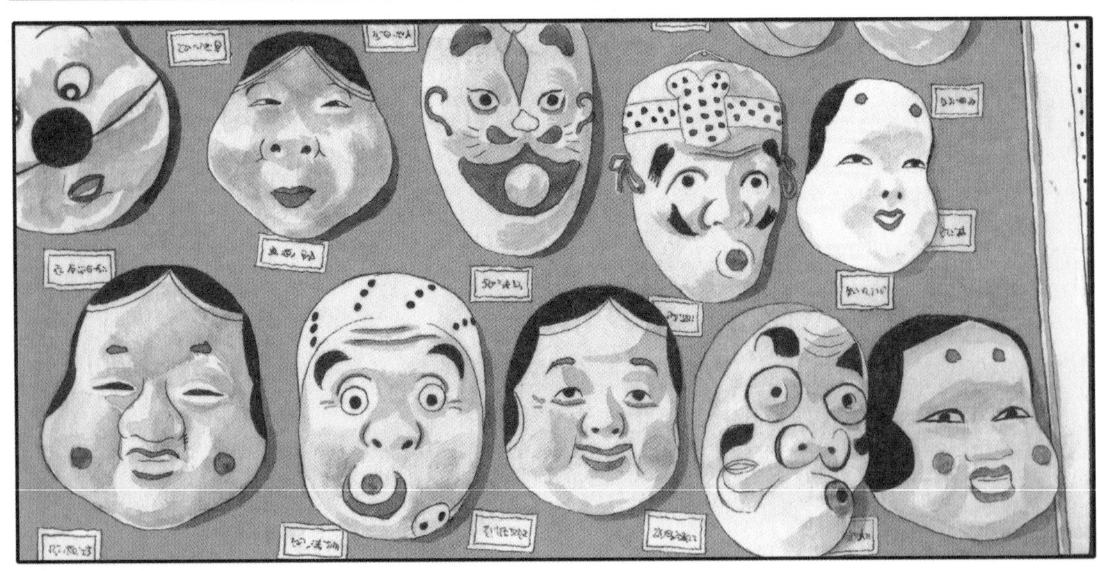

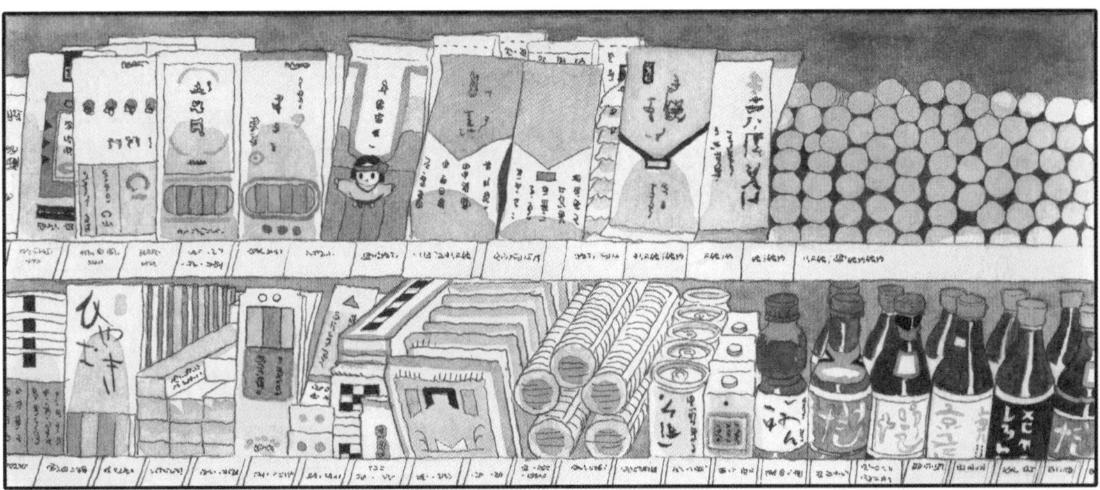

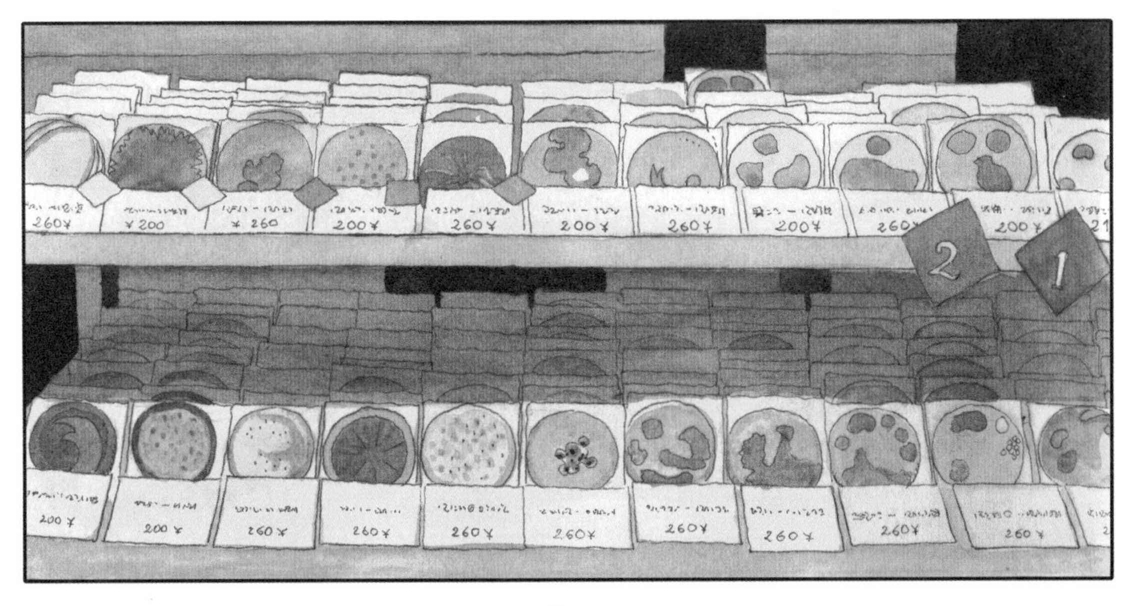
260¥
¥200
¥260
200¥
260¥
200¥
260¥
200¥
260¥
200¥
2
1
200¥
200¥
260¥
260¥
260¥
260¥
260¥
260¥
260¥
260¥

1994. Gardenia House, apartment 101, Sendagi ni-Chome, Bunkyo-Ku. Here I am in Tokyo to draw my comics, with a contract in my pocket from the biggest publisher in the Land of the Rising Sun.

I lived in a small, 150-square-foot apartment. Now and then I'd look out the window and observe the plum tree in bloom, in that Japanese spring. It was a very old area, Bunkyo-Ku, composed of small buildings and filled with temples and shrines.

They protected the Imperial Palace from bad spirits.

Which as everyone knows travel from northeast to southwest.

And then, immersed in that silence, I would lose myself for hours drawing or taking notes. From Tokyo, Europe, my regular life, truly seemed far away.

"The life source of the human body is qi. When you are in a state of peace, you preserve your basic energy, when you are in movement you make it circulate. Preservation and circulation. If you don't have these two characteristics, it will be difficult for you to cultivate qi."

Tofu was delivered by a guy on a bicycle who rode through the side streets of my neighborhood. He would announce his arrival by sounding his horn.

I had my beloved fresh tofu!

"Your mind should always be composed, serene, at peace. You shouldn't talk about useless things. This is the best way to preserve qi."

I usually took the subway to get around. In 1994, when I decided to take my first bus, headed for Kodansha, I had been living in Sendagi for a few weeks. As opposed to the subway, on the bus you can't see the name of the next stop and can only rely on the loudspeaker announcement. Through eleven long stops I kept saying to myself, "if you get off at the wrong stop you're in trouble. You don't speak Japanese, you can't read ideograms, you've been reduced to the state of primitive man. You won't know where you are and getting back will be a disaster."

I remember sweating with tension. And I strained my ear to decipher those ceremoniously uttered guttural sounds. When I finally heard the recorded voice say: "Otowa Ni-Chome degozaimasu" my knees were shaking. I got off the 58. I had arrived.

To me, Japan had become a treasure chest filled with all kinds of things, but especially this: an artist's paradise. Intoxicated by old Japanese prints, I had penetrated that world of signs, which was apparently simple but contained mysterious knowledge.

A drawing made with rapid brushstrokes, seeming to trace forms invisible to regular mortals.

How did they do it?

"Pictures of the floating world," as they were called, offered a way of seeing nature that always remained unreachable, helping to create that aura of legend that has endured up to today.

Besides the masters revered in the West (Hiroshige, Hokusai, Utamaro) there were others, less well known, who had a hypnotic power over me. One of them was Sharaku, whose portraits of kabuki actors took my breath away.

But earlier, 10 years before, when I first got Japan fever, my visions were different. I drew Japan during wartime.

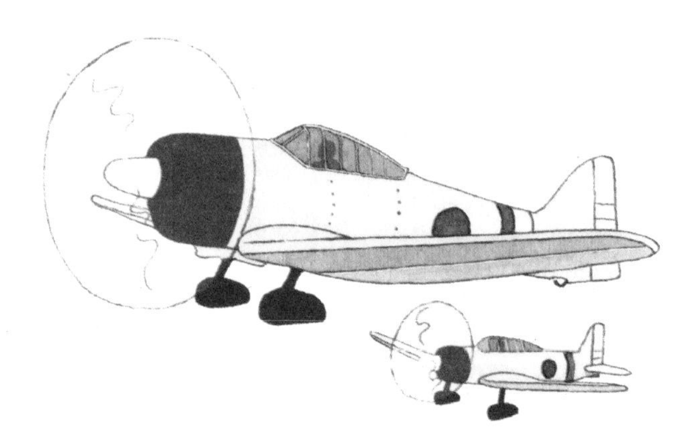

The Showa period. In Japanese, Showa Jidai, which means literally "period of enlightened peace."

WOOOOOOOOOOOOOOOO

Only yesterday . . .

DRIIN DRIIN DRIIN

This is my mother. In the sweltering summer of 1980, I spent several intense days working in Sardinia, at my parents' house, following the flow of those visions that came to me one after the other.

Hiro Oolong, head of the Nippon imperial butchery in Parador.

A past he would like to forget.

A pain that keeps on renewing itself.

Sleepless nights spent listening to Mahler.

I told the story of a man of glass at the mercy of his obsessions and morbidly in love with meat.

I had read Roland Barthes's "Empire of Signs," his travelogue about Japan composed of fragments.

The epigraph to the book advised: "The text does not 'gloss' the images, which do not 'illustrate' the text." A declaration of poetics, "modern" and open, that privileged insight. Enlightening.

For some time, I had been playing with the idea of a long story composed of "suggestions of the intimate and the unsaid."

So I started working on the new story, pulling out a random card after Brian Eno's model. "Oblique Strategies," the English musician called them.

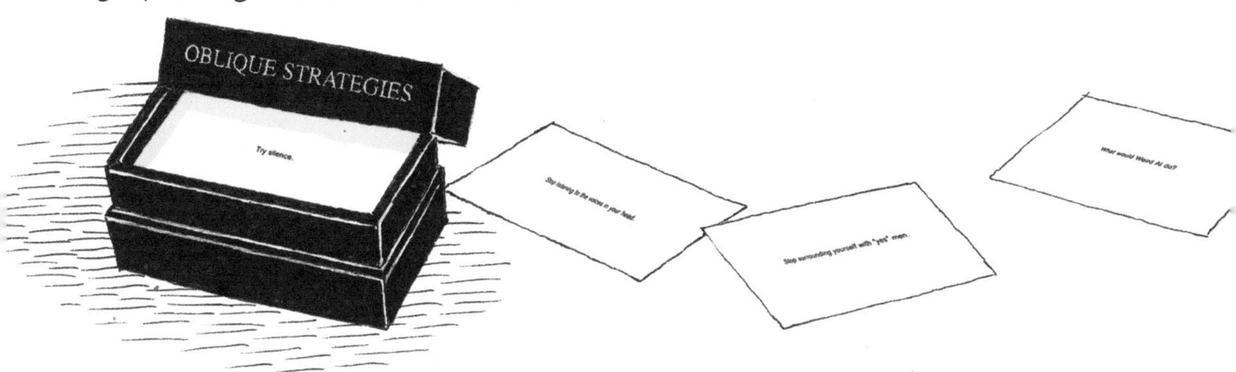

Basically, Eno seemed to believe that chance could guide us if we listened to it.

Each card had abstract suggestions, like "go with the flow," or random suggestions to use for guiding composition. An almost divinatory method inspired by the practices in the great book of changes, the "I-Ching."

Chance, which was so celebrated by the Dadaists, became my guide for constructing a story. Within a few days I had made my own cards. They said things like: "outside, daytime, two people talking, one of them has a secret," or "traveling, an unexpected occurrence," or "above and below, meanwhile."

I built a narrative framework. It was a method that made me happy and enabled me to play as I was writing. Excellent for my qi. Ekiken would have been pleased.

Daniele was Daniele Brolli, a writer and cartoonist friend, who helped to flesh out the plot and make it more visionary.

And that was our first long comic, or graphic novel, as they're called today. A hundred pages or so, published in magazines and later as a single volume.

It was in that same period that I found an English version of the precepts of Ekiken, my beloved seventeenth-century samurai doctor. "If you eat, drink, and have sex in moderation, keep set hours for sleeping and being awake, and take care of yourself, you will never get sick," assured Ekiken.

He was also a noted botanist and wrote a seminal tract on medicinal herbs, which he catalogued in his "Yamato Honzo."

He was a fervent supporter of the majesty of nature. He said that when there were storms or wind storms, you should sit down and receive them, even if it was the dead of night.

"An ancient saying has it that patience is the jewel of the body. If you can be patient, you will not be unhappy; if you cannot be patient, you will be unhappy. Patience is a matter of self-control."

Ten years later, there I was.

The first time I set foot in the Kodansha building, from the 1930s, it was May 1991.

My collaboration with the biggest publishing house in the Land of the Rising Sun began almost by chance, like in a spy movie.
At the Bologna Book Fair, at the Kodansha stand, I was chatting with Yuka Ando, head of foreign rights. I said that I thought Japan should consider doing collaborations between Japanese and European authors.
It was the moment. I was absolutely sure about it.
I saw her flush. "Did I say something wrong?" I wondered.
Without saying another word, she motioned for me to follow her into the private office in the back of the stand.
She told me: "We're working on a secret project between Otomo and Jodorowsky, how did you know?"

Actually, I didn't know, but that's how I learned that my idea was shared by others. One month later I was in Tokyo, and I was nurturing a dream: to create long stories.

Yuka met me at the historic Kodansha offices, the same ones where Mishima saw his editors. Then she led me to the separate office of the Seventh division, where she introduced me to the director, Kurihara San.

I had never seen such a large staff at a comics magazine. There were 55 editors.

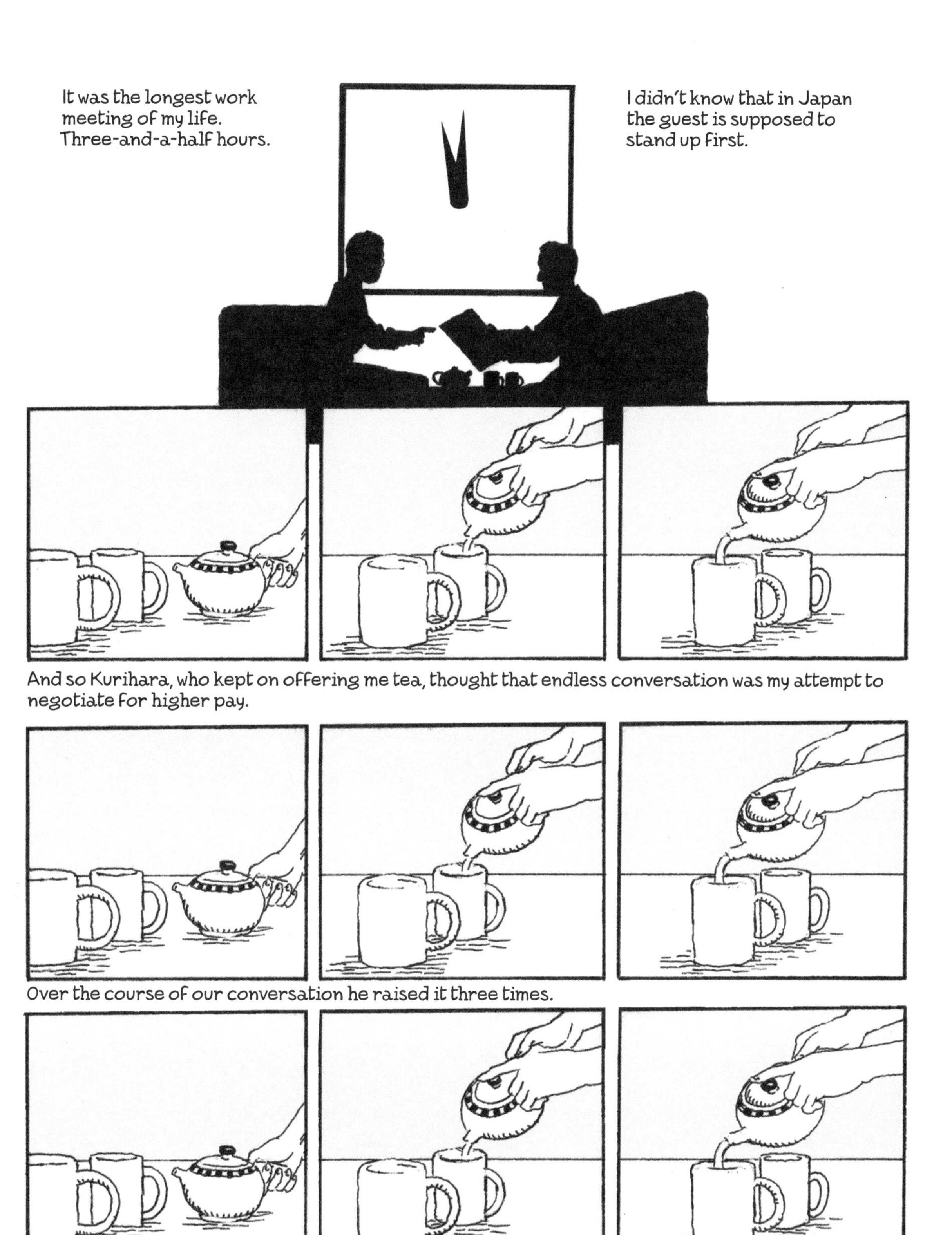
It was the longest work meeting of my life. Three-and-a-half hours.
I didn't know that in Japan the guest is supposed to stand up first.
And so Kurihara, who kept on offering me tea, thought that endless conversation was my attempt to negotiate for higher pay.
Over the course of our conversation he raised it three times.
As they say, the fortune of not fully knowing the customs of a place.

That was the exact moment when my second life began. I had been publishing in Europe for years. And I thought I knew what I wanted to do, say, draw. But I was wrong. Three years later I was awarded the Morning Manga Fellowship, and I was invited to go and live in Tokyo, for a month up to a year. Now that was a prize. I decided to stay for six months.

Obviously it was my entrance into a new world, a universe made of indecipherable rules that at the time were mind-boggling and fascinating.

And obviously my relationship with space also changed.

It was little more than a dollhouse, 150 square feet. I soon learned to draw at a tiny desk.

But I adapted quickly. New spaces and new habits. I spent days and nights intent at the table, drawing and arranging ideas, organizing that flood of stories I'd been dreaming about for years and that now was finally within reach. In Europe, comic albums were 60 pages long. The phenomenon of the graphic novel was not widespread.

The first project I did for Kodansha was called "Amore." A story set in Sicily telling the life story of Mario Bongiorno, the son of a mafia boss who refused to get into the family business. He wanted a carefree life, liked women (hence the nickname "Love"); he was a bit of a braggart, who in the movies would have been played by Marcello Mastroianni.

Obviously I had to learn to draw in the opposite direction, since in Japan they read from right to left. It wasn't that complicated. We're more adaptable than we think.

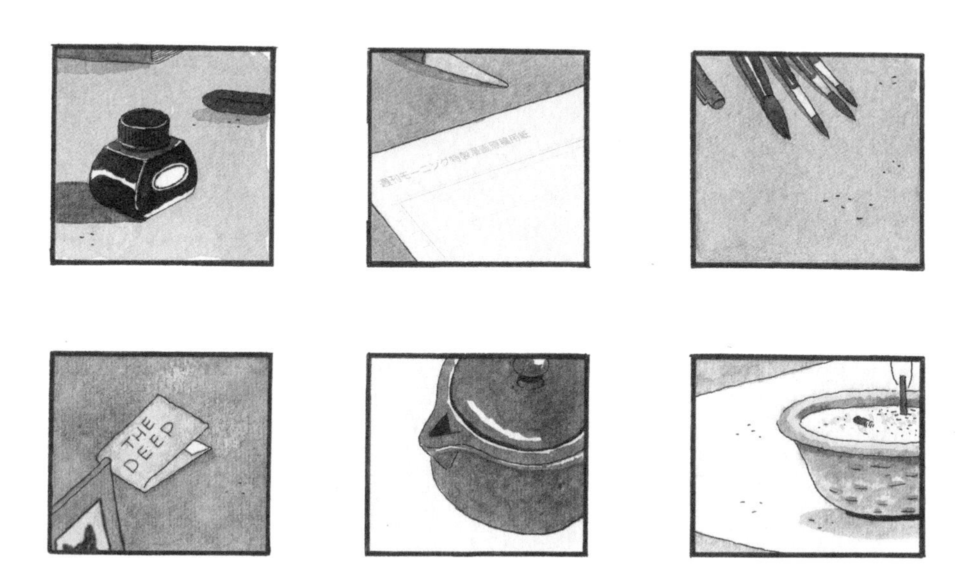

I would wake up at first light. I slept on the floor, on a futon that folded up in the closet, as they used to do in traditional Japanese houses. By 5:40 I was already out, heading for my Zen refuge.

While Tokyo was still asleep, I was walking down Dangozaka Dori up to Yanaka, passing by Tennoji Temple.

I would stop there for a moment to observe the monks sweeping circles around the trees. Silent, completely focused. Those gardens were purely the fruit of their spiritual exercises.

Then I went on to Takuboku Dojo, my Zen school Rinzai, which had become a home, a place of comfort. In the morning there was hardly anyone in the gigantic meditation room. The sounds of the wood and the bells echoed, then five minutes of silence. A 10 minute break followed by another 45 minute session.

I had brought some books by Mishima with me. After a long period of neglect in Europe, they started reprinting his work in the '80s.

Mishima, a true Japanese icon, had come to a tragic fate. He died a violent death. He left an ode to a disappearing Japan.

Faithful to the samurai honor code, the Bushido, he took his life in ritual suicide after taking the commandant of defense prisoner and delivering a speech to the military on the decline of Japan.

Dismissed by the ignorant left as a petty fascist, to me Mishima seemed fragile, a creature of glass like a Tennessee Williams character, a kaleidoscope of visions and poetic contradictions. Too complex for an ideological reading, too subtle for a superficial reading.

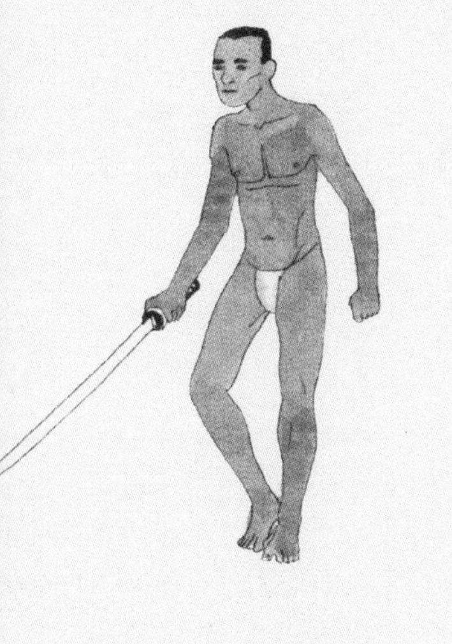

After his tragic death, Alberto Moravia and Norman Mailer wrote about him. But hara-kiri, that so distant and incomprehensible act, was seen as the sign of a strange and indecipherable depression.

Yet Marguerite Yourcenar penned some unforgettable lines, dense and full of humanity.

After all, she was the author of "Memoirs of Hadrian," a tribute to empathy.

Thus, word after word, page by page, breathing in unison with that martyred soul like a great novelist, she probed his idiosyncrasies, investigated his contradictions without any preconceptions. She made that jumble of seemingly inextricable knots clear, comprehensible, and human. Revealing to all of us a man in the splendor of his poetic dream.

A man overtaken by the ecstasy of the flesh. Who appealed to traditional Japanese values yet ate with Western utensils rather than the proverbial chopsticks, who lived in a multi-story art nouveau house, having left his tatami house to his parents.

Who adhered to Bushido code, the samurai way of the warrior, but refused to pay homage to the emperor, whom he considered guilty of surrender.

Mishima talked to Kami, the spirits central to Shintoism, and derided kamikazes, who died for a child of God (the Emperor) who had forgotten his nature.

Mishima was difficult, controversial, not beyond censure, but also deeply alive and essential to an intellectual debate that made beauty and sacrifice into two poles by which to titanically elevate the world.

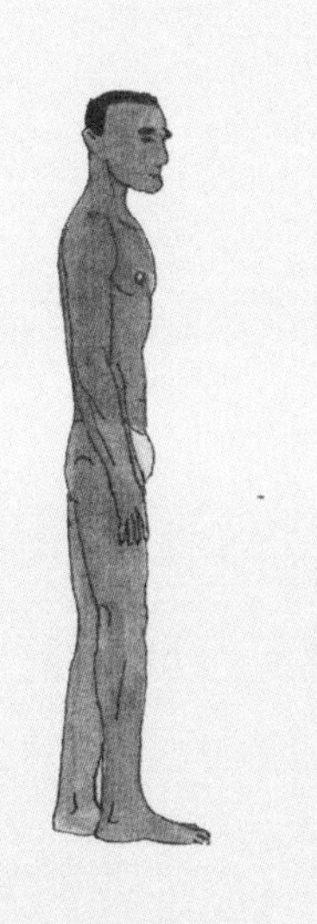

My Japan was also Mishima, tormented by his demons no less than Hokusai or Mizuki—but they'll come up later.

I ate once a day and quickly lost 12 kilos. In fact, I was called in to Kodansha by the big boss, who was worried that I was unhappy or unwell in Japan.

Actually, it was one of the happiest periods of my life. I drew until late listening on my headphones to the Ramones and Led Zeppelin, who for some reason sounded very different in Japan. In the mornings I would study Japanese and have my tea, then set out on half-empty streets. In the narrow side streets of Bunkyo-Ku, far from the noise on Shinobazu Dori, the neighborhood seemed asleep, closed in a timeless bubble.

500
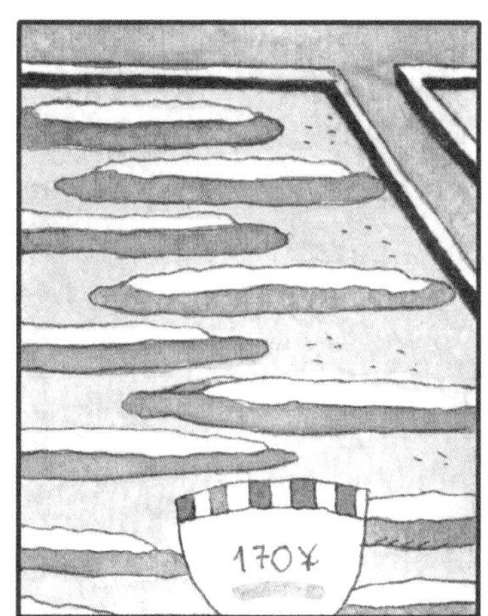
170¥

DIN DIN

Almost every author had multiple assistants in order to handle their weekly assignments.

We spent a couple of hours discussing how the machine of paper dreams worked in Japan and in Europe. Manga and comics, two reflecting worlds. We talked about the most banal things, like how many hours we worked a day, our relationships with editors, what life was like in Europe. Jiro San was a curious and attentive listener.

He showed me how he worked, I met his assistants, and saw his studio, packed with papers, books, and projects, paint, documentary photos.

That meeting was the first of many. We established a friendship that grew over the years. We would see each other all over: Tokyo, Paris, Bologna, Angoulême.
Little by little as our lives went on.

Through our common editor I also met Tanaka San, the author of "Gon," a hugely successful manga published in the magazine "Comic Morning."

Gon was a baby tyrannosaurus. His stories, set in nature, were finely drawn, and had an element that set them apart: they were completely wordless.

When we'd been successful, we'd take a much-needed break at a restaurant, Kodansha's treat. Tanaka would choose his dishes based on price, ordering only the most expensive things.

Tsutsumi Yasumitsu was my editor. A cultured, intelligent, and disciplined man, who conceived of his work as collaboration. He didn't like to impose his own ideas, but rather used the Socratic method. What the Greeks called "maieutics," the art of arriving at deep truths through dialogue.

And he would ask me, why this? Why that?

With him, I learned many things about my own world, what I was looking for, what the themes of my work as a storyteller were.

Obviously it wasn't all moonlight and roses. Our relationship was even turbulent at times. All the way through the "treatment." But that will come up later, when I tell you about the second series I created for Kodansha.

The first series, "Amore," was a story set in Sicily. I had fun with it, using a very cinematic perspective, which heightened the dramatic effect of the particularly brutal scenes.

39

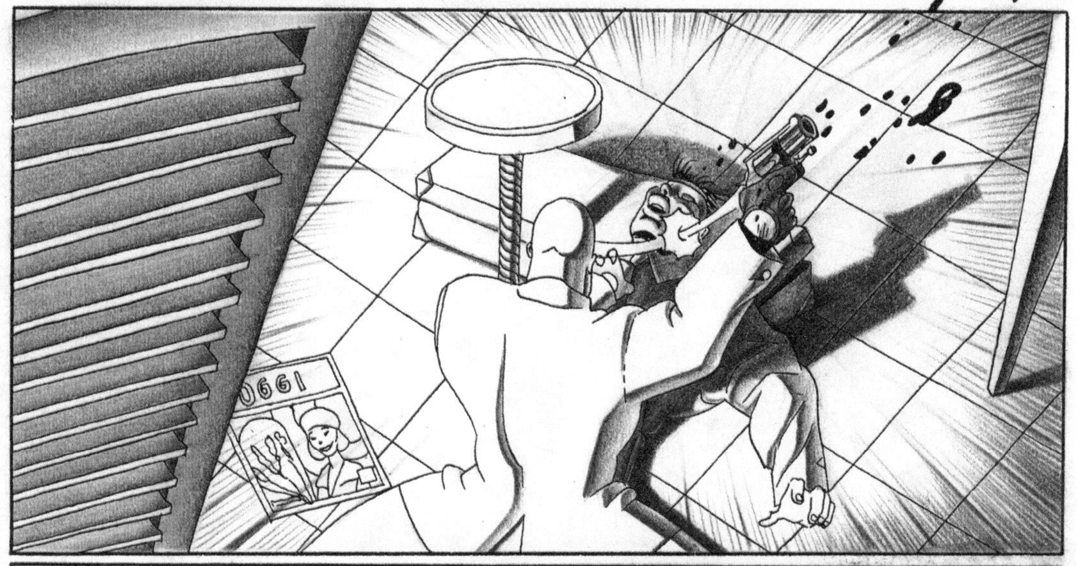

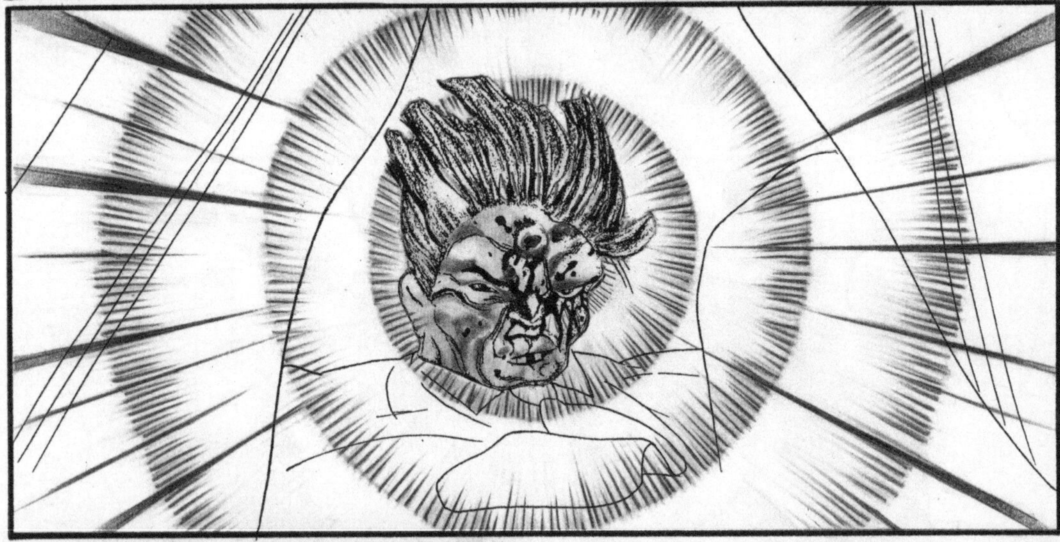
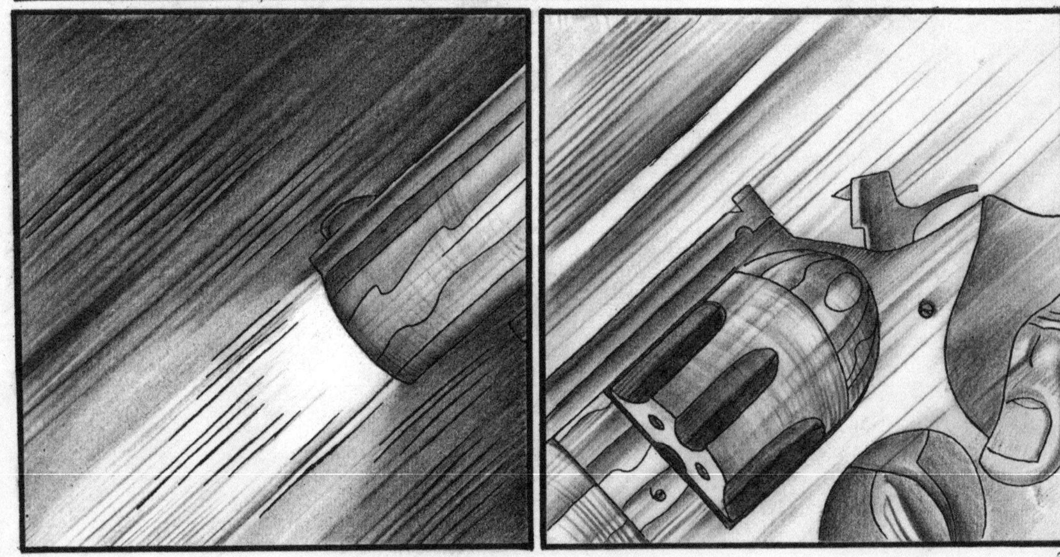

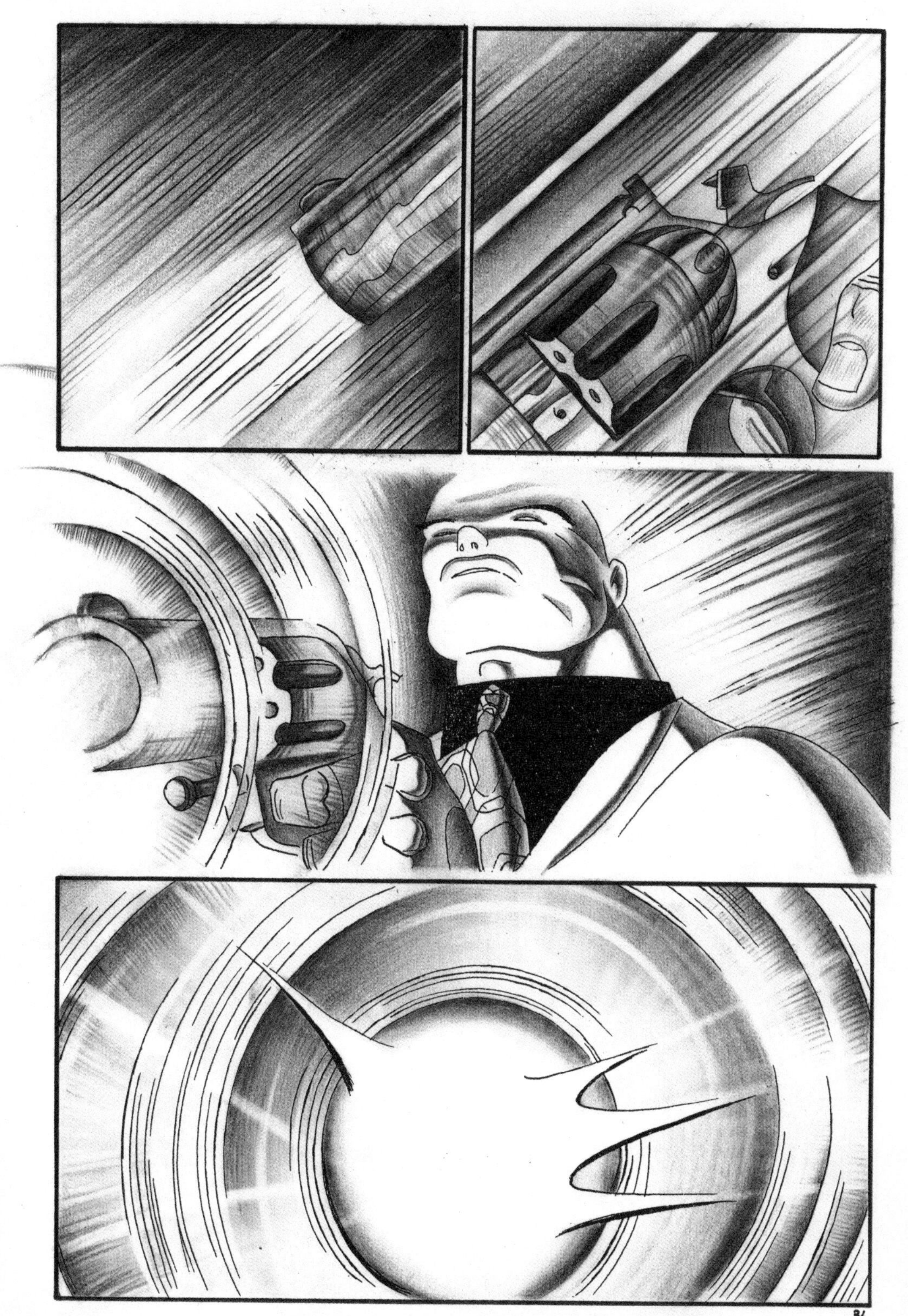

To depict the violence of the Italian mafia, I hit the gas on the sequences and dynamic effects. Tsutsumi, upon learning about my spiritual explorations, made fun of me: "Eh, I know. Even vegetarians like blood."

I loved the genre movies produced in Japan by great directors who were virtually unknown in the West. Directors who had worked in B movies, like those produced by Nikkatsu, which continually cranked out Yakuza, samurai, and erotic movies, called "pinku eiga" or "pink" films.

I looked for movies by Suzuki, Misumi, and Imamura.

My friendship with the great editor Hajime Tamiya was cemented by the movies of Beat Takeshi Kitano and Seijun Suzuki, whom we both loved.

Tamiya was a genius. The editor of "Akira," the director of "Jump Magazine," whom I secretly signed up for karaoke to make him sing Elvis. He was up for it, surprised at getting called to the stage, and secretly amused at my total impertinence.

He was also director of the Third editorial division of Kodansha, and in Japan roles are respected positions honored.

One night, while I was excitedly going on about "Branded to Kill" (Koroshi no rakuin), directed by Seijun Suzuki, with its wonderfully stylized port scenes, he asked me: "Why don't you write a manga for us?"

By "us" he meant for the Third division, which was a competitor of the Seventh, the one I worked for. He had already tried to ask me in the past, but the magazine editors chewed him out. They didn't even like our being friends. That made me mad; I choose my own friends without any need for a godfather. And he and I had a special understanding, ever since the time he was my guest in Bologna and had asked to go to the racetrack, to play the horses. And since, when he couldn't find the bathroom in the gigantic house I was renting, so as not to wake me up he urinated on one of his T-shirts that he later put in a bag and threw away.

So, after more than a year, I did the story "Amore," inspired by the films we both loved. It was published shortly before his death. He died at 55. How can that be?

very time I think of him I feel melancholy, then I laugh to myself, remembering him at karaoke.

eijun Suzuki. Days spent searching for his films. Even copies of copies, just to see how he irected, told his stories, before finally being able to buy the DVDs in France, in the HK Video set. he legend of Seijun Suzuki had reached Europe. A talented and original director, who also shot our or five Yakuza movies a year, with a wonderful visionary imagination. A master adored by arantino and Kitano.

ver the years his style became more and more personal and eccentric, until "Branded to Kill," ilmed in 1967, brought him to his peak.

e was after pure cinema. Geometrically choreographed shootouts, silences, sudden music, and ontinual visual inventions, like the idea of getting rid of setting. His characters moved in an bstract, metaphysical space.

was too much for the heads at Nikkatsu, the film house he had always worked for, who fired him on he spot. Then for a time his work disappeared and his career ended abruptly.

Japan I combed the little thrift stores looking for his films. But it wasn't easy. When I talked bout Seijun Suzuki people didn't seem to know him. They'd heard of a few titles: "Youth of the east" (Yajû No Seishun), "Gate of Flesh" (Nikutai no Mon), "Tokyo Drifter" (Tokyo Nagaremono), r "Branded to Kill," but didn't know who directed them. Actually, they seemed taken aback that a esterner, a "gaijin," was so interested in those old B movies. Things they didn't put much stock in.

A small homage to Seijun Suzuki's "Branded to Kill" (Koroshi no rakuin), 1967.

Sendagi 1 Chome, one day in May.

I don't know why, but I'd gotten myself a brick red jacket.

It had seemed like a good idea, but evidently I was wrong.

At any rate, I crossed Sendagi 1 Chome to the Nezu Shrine almost every day.

On that initiatory trip, I had learned to hug trees, which welcomed me at Nezu from the heights of their age-old majesty.

I can't say that I expected to be alone. In reality I didn't mind if anyone saw me. They could think whatever they wanted. Nezu-Jinja was a Shinto shrine. And the Shinto religion contemplates nature, no?
I had crossed Japan far and wide in search of my master. I hadn't found him, but in those wanderings I once spotted a Shinto priest performing his ritual.

It was forbidden, but I watched the middle-aged man anyway . . .

. . . singing, completely underwater,

. . . inspired and absorbed.

The days passed in that new state of mind. I soon learned to appreciate the intimate, reserved aspect of things. Although Tokyo was a megalopolis of almost nine million people, the structure of the city maintained the dimension of a group of villages.

I lived in Sendagi, in a neighborhood that looked very ancient, where the writer Natsume Soseki had lived.

That city had a gift for calming me, of depositing sand on the seabed of my existence.

I listened attentively.
1

Very far from home, but still on an island, I searched for the meaning of my existence. And immersed in the beauty of the azalea gardens cultivated by diligent monks with otherworldly care, surrounded by ancient trees, at moments I felt like I grasped it, that meaning.

Then it slipped away, like water between my fingers.

I kept repeating this to myself.

Three centuries have passed since this shrine was founded . . .

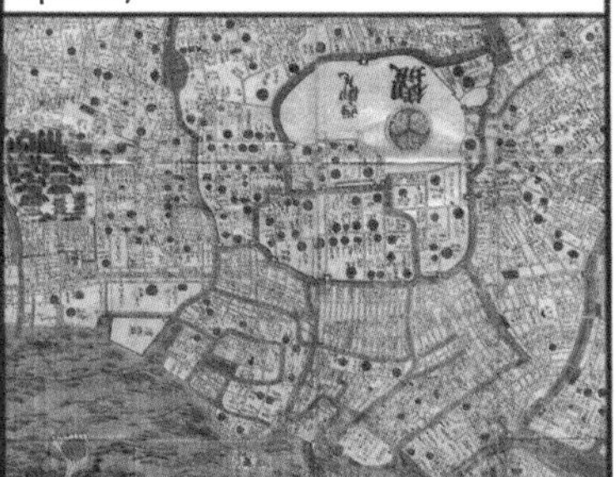
. . . and although Tokyo had changed around it at a dizzying speed,

in that place, time seemed to flow at a different pace.

I breathed deeply.

Yes, maybe that's what Nezu was to me, the luxury of self-care, of allowing myself deep breaths that came unexpectedly.

飛行機

10

軍旗

50

傳書鳩

90

大將

60

I had convinced myself and my editors at Kodansha that I was Japanese in a past life. They greeted me ceremoniously, bowing. "We Japanese are honored to work with you, who in turn, in your previous life, were Japanese." I loved these people, wry and mild-mannered, but devoted to work with a rigor I'd never seen before. During that trip Japan fever started to envelop me, under the guise of a sweet melancholy. I was saddened by the ancient beauty of this or that wooden house and rice paper that I noticed now and then in my neighborhood. It spoke of a remote era.

That was the Japan I was seeing evaporate before my eyes, blown away by the hectic bustle of modern life.

So, for pleasure and to assuage that feeling, I would go to my favorite bookstore in the Jimbocho quarter, a huge eight-story building with old books, photos, manga, film posters ('60s westerns were my favorite, with the cowboys and Indians played by Japanese actors, amazing stuff!).

And after admiring the drawing style of the images, which the Japanese have nothing to envy from anyone, I would buy dozens of faded postcards and Menko cards. Menkos were playing cards illustrated with heroes from manga or popular myths (samurais, sumo wrestlers, war heroes, and later, baseball players).

In those colors, printed on third-rate paper, I could see the connection between Japanese prints and Western pop icons.

Captivated, I would go back to Gardenia House on the subway, a 45-minute trip that lasted an instant, lulled by the images that I would draw in my notebooks later at home.

The myth of the warrior has been passed down through centuries of Japanese culture and has been represented with infinite grace in millions of images. They had come to us with a diabolical mix of fascination and death. I spent hours looking at those images.

To understand what a strange people the Japanese were, during the war the American government asked an anthropologist, Ruth Benedict, to shed some light on their culture.

She wrote a memorable book, "The Chrysanthemum and the Sword," published in 1946, where she attempts to explain that normal Western categories of "logic" were an insufficient tool for understanding.

The book described how grace and the cult of beauty overlapped with the cult of strength and death. And that there was nothing unusual about this according to Nipponese tradition.

萬
國
國

Kiku, chrysanthemum.

Chrysanthemums were grown as a pastime even by samurai.
The emperor Gotoba Tenno (1138-1198) also loved them for their beauty, making them his family symbol.
The Japanese aristocracy began to appreciate that flower, symbol of peace, longevity, and nobility of spirit.
Eventually Chrysanthemum Day, Kiku no Sekku, was established, which falls on the ninth day of the ninth month, so every September 9.
The flowers bloomed with the first frost, and it was believed that this concluded the active and creative period of the year. A seal, essentially.
Kaoru San, the Ikebana teacher I meet at Nishi Nippori, is especially fond of it.
It's my favorite, that flower. Maybe because it's tied to my family history. My father would tell me:
Look closely at the chrysanthemum. It's like a sun with rays of light. Do you see them?
Yes, papa.
The history of the chrysanthemum has been intertwined with Japan's for centuries, at least since—although some native exemplars existed—a select species was imported from China, over a thousand years ago.

The symbol of a sun with sixteen long, graphic petals can still be found today at the entrance to the Yasukuni Shrine.

For the celebration, the ninth day of the ninth month, courtesans paraded through the pleasure district. And the pleasure houses displayed vases of chrysanthemums at the entrance.

The procession led to a shrine dedicated to Inari, the fox spirit, a symbol of femininity, where people prayed for enduring youth and long and happy lives.

With the growing popularity of the flower, they started making life-sized human figures called Kiku Ningyo (literally, chrysanthemum dolls).

They were made by building a light frame out of woven reeds or wire on which the flowers were grown like a robe. Then the head, hands, and feet were formed out of wax and realistically colored. You often saw the face of a famous actor from kabuki theater. Tickets for these shows were usually very expensive, given the high costs of producing these dolls life-sized. Unfortunately, this custom has mostly disappeared.

The idea that the chrysanthemum symbolizes long life comes from the fact that it can grow in desert areas, survive in the cold, and doesn't lose its petals, even when it wilts. Kaoru San offers me some cookies and pulls out a book in English. "Please read this; you can give it back to me before you leave."

The emperor celebrated chrysanthemums so the dwindling autumn sunlight wouldn't cause people's vital energy to drop.

In Japan there is an ancient healing tradition that consists of placing cotton balls on chrysanthemums on September 8, the eve of the holiday.

The following morning, the cotton, damp with dew, is used to clean the body; this custom of purification is known as the "chrysanthemum cotton treatment."

I often went to Ryugoku, the sumo district. Sometimes, I'd see one of the wrestlers in the flesh coming out of a chanko restaurant or a beya after practice. He would shuffle calmly down the street in his robe, followed by a trail of strong cologne. I would end up discreetly following behind, noticing the restrained excitement his presence created among passersby. The people who recognized him couldn't help but congratulate him. For my part, I observed silently. It's not easy to speak with demigods. Not on the same level, at least. On my trips, year after year, my curiosity about the sumo world intensified. Folklore gave way to studying the fundamentals, its tradition, the deep meaning it holds.

Dating back to the sixth century, sumo came out of the Shinto spiritual tradition, and still maintains its propitiatory rituals. Shiko, for example, that characteristic motion of lifting one leg and then the other, may look like a stretch, but is actually for driving away evil spirits.

And throwing salt, which they do several times during matches, is a talisman for avoiding injuries or bad falls.

Thus, when my agent, Yamada San, asked me what I'd like to do in Tokyo, I told him I'd like to see a training session. He took me to the Nihonbashi district, near a gym.

Out back there were some sumo wrestlers stretching in the sun, moving slowly because of their bulk, and they played around, splashing each other. They quickly revealed themselves for what they really were: little boys in overgrown bodies. And yet they emanated that ancient allure that we don't have in the West. A battle where a match lasts just a few minutes, composed of balance, sudden shifts in weight, in the attempt to throw off the opponent, get him out of the ring.

When I was younger, I told the story of melancholy sumotori Hiro Oolong, and that character had gotten under my skin. Almost thirty years later, I would return to his story, starting with his childhood.

And now here they were in front of me, in the flesh, all these Hiro Oolongs. Warming up, perfumed, oiled and shiny, under the Tokyo sun.

Through the years my relationship with Kodansha and my editor grew, and I would come to Japan and stay at the Fairmont, a hotel near the Kudanshita station, across from the artificial lake surrounding the emperor's palace.

I came with my work materials: this would become my studio for a month, a month and a half, depending. I went back every year.

When I was subjected to what I'll call "the treatment," it was 1996, and I had been working in Japan for several years. My second series, "Yuri," was published in "Comic Morning," which sold 1,400,000 copies a week.

I got in at eight in the morning, Japan time, which in my time zone was midnight. I thought I would be able to go and rest.

But that was not the case, because my editor, who had kindly come with two other colleagues to collect me, took me to the Fairmont and said: "If you'd like to take a shower, we'll wait for you in the lobby."

At first I didn't understand.

It seemed like they wanted to give me an even more ceremonious welcome.

But I was wrong, because when I went down to the lobby a half hour later, although I was spiritually ready to put on my pajamas, we got down to work. Following his motto, "an author is a character's best biographer," Tsutsumi San began asking me questions.

I was tired and unfocused, I muttered out banalities. I hadn't expected to be subjected to that sort of test. I didn't even understand the reason for it.

Then I noticed that one of the other editors wasn't talking, but frantically taking notes, not taking his eyes off his notepad.

Our pitiful welcome meeting ended after a couple of hours of pure torment in which, I fully realized, I had made a bunch of uninteresting comments about the personality of my most popular character.

Yuri had been published the entire previous season, earning a certain amount of success with the public. Readers, asked to vote on their favorite character, had responded favorably.

The young editors in charge of lettering often exclaimed "kawaii" (cute). And about 500 postcards and fan letters had come.

It was important and exciting. When my translator, Midori Yamane, sent me a long fax with the translated letters, I stared open-mouthed waiting for it to finish. But the paper kept coming and coming. What I hadn't at all expected was that Japanese readers would participate so actively. Not only did they follow Yuri's story, but rooted him on like a real person. They suggested ideas, other characters. One four-year-old, via one of his parents, requested an underwater adventure. So I did one. Another suggested I draw a boy robot called Mora.

Before Tsutsumi San said goodbye, he tried—in his way—to motivate me to face that challenge, which turned out to be the toughest I had ever had. But I didn't know that the worst was yet to come.

Kokoro, Igoruto San, we have to reach the hearts of the readers.

When we tiredly parted ways and I thought I had earned the right to rest and recuperate, he said this enigmatic phrase, in a completely offhanded way.

I believe I shut my eyes for three hours, maximum, and then I sat down at the table.

Then, as always happens when you're in a corner, at a certain point the story poured out. It flashed in front of me. And I began to transcribe it.

In less than two hours I was drawing.

I thought back to Tsutsumi San's advice.
Remember, the character must always have a frame. If he is hidden, the reader must know where he is.
And you need unity of time and action.
I faxed the text to Midori at four in the morning, who translated it in real time and sent it to Tokyo by opening time. Eight o'clock in the morning, Japan.
Good morning, Mr. Tanaka, I need to send a fax to Italy.
After two hours, at 10, Tsutsumi San knocked on my door.
Good morning, Tsutsumi San.
Konnichiwa.

He had read the story, scrutinized the pages. Not a single muscle on his face gave away his reaction. After about 10 minutes, he said:

Tomorrow, another.

I lay down but couldn't relax. I was in Tokyo, but I could have been anywhere, since it was impossible to go out. A flurry of emotions rapidly went through me: frustration, depression, anger. I went to buy some sandwiches and brought them back to my room.

began to understand that my editors had taken the idea that I'd been Japanese like them in a past life seriously. The legends about the working conditions in the world of manga had ricocheted all the way to Europe.

met him, Go Nagai, at a Kodansha party. The old Japanese master, upon learning that I was working in the manga industry, put his hand on my shoulder and said, smiling:

*Good luck

The second was another nearly sleepless night, writing and drawing. I remember taking advantage of the favorable time change and calling Italy. Alberto, a doctor friend.

Alberto, listen, I have Yuri in the snow, buried in an avalanche. How long could he last if he's wearing a thermal snowsuit?

TOC
TOC

I got technical responses that helped me to make my stories believable: Midori, in Rome, waited for the text, and while I finished drawing she would translate them and fax them to Tokyo. The Japanese teamwork machine on the job.

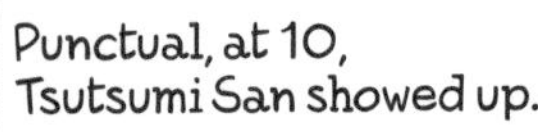

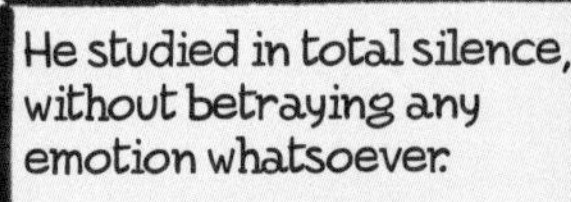

My anger mounted. It wasn't so much the work that got to me but his laconic comment. He didn't say whether he liked the stories or not, and being long used to discussion, I was disoriented, tired, furious.

By that point I was seeing double, even though I allowed myself an hour of fresh air a day, which I used to go out first thing in the morning and have breakfast at the kissaten around the corner with a muffin and hot cocoa, and then five hours later to refuel with sandwiches for lunch and dinner.

My anger at Tsutsumi San grew. To unwind, I would mentally picture his visit the next morning. I imagined greeting him with a punch in the face, before hearing him say yet again "tomorrow, another."

Mon-do are riddles, seemingly meaningless sentences that masters say in order to stimulate growth in their pupil's consciousness. To help them reach enlightenment.

Then he added:

It's too soon to quit. You must continue, Igoruto San.

And I continued. I did 160 pages in two weeks, with a four day break, to catch my breath.

And then we tossed everything. Of the letters that kept arriving during the publication of the first series, 90% complimented the color. "We can't do a new series in black and white," Tsutsumi San said. "The audience wants warm colors, but we have only eight pages of space for color. I'm sorry." And so it went.

QUANTE STORIE FARE IL BAGNO OGNI TANTO TI FA BENE
PENSA CHE ERO PRONTO A COMBATTERE, PERCHE SAI CI SONO G INVASO
IO SONO UNO DI LORO
UN ATTIMO CHE MI ALLACCIO IL GIUBOTTO E TU YURI COSA ASPETTI?
YURI ! FROM MARS WITH LOVE
YURI
IL PRIMO BIMBO ASTRA
BUNA SERRA
OH. BUON GIORNO
GIORNO
SPLOOSH
AAAH. ARIA. MALATO GRAVE CHE SONO A ALL'ACQUA. BISOGNO DI!
A CAUSA DELLA SUA INCOMPETENZA DEVO SEMPRE FARE IL BAGNO...

When I went with my friend Mikiko to get teacups, the man who had made them told me that new cups may be pretty, but with use little cracks would form inside. Those cracks, forming a delicate spiderweb, marked the passage of time. That, he told me, was the beauty of an object. I couldn't help but think of Junichiro Tanizaki's wonderful "In Praise of Shadows."

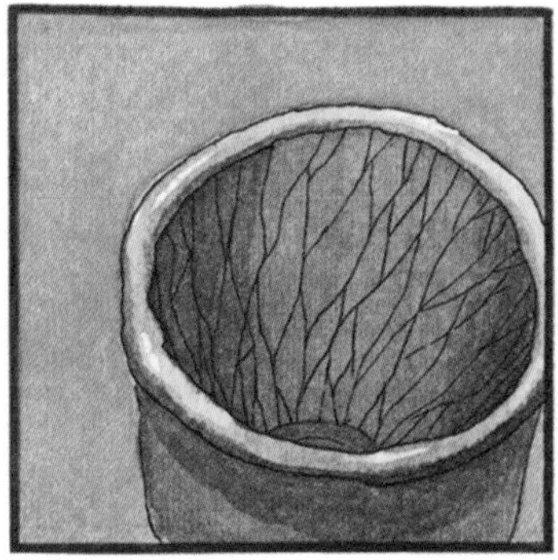

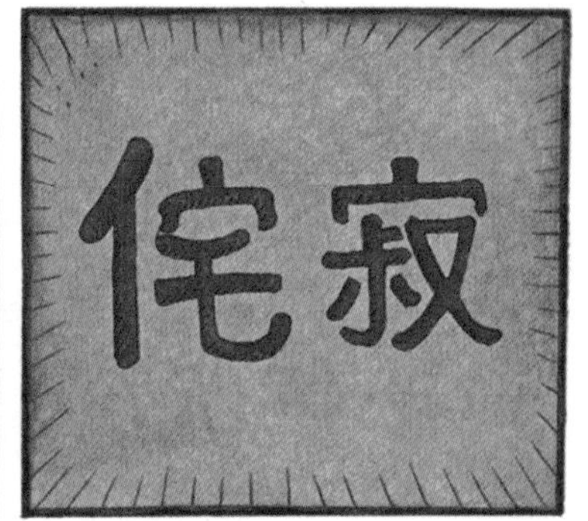

Read and reread in my youth, loved and adored. The essay, written by Tanizaki in 1933, is an analytic journey through the world of beauty, a celebration of obscurity, shadow, penumbra, in all of its manifestations. I read it as an initiation to that fluctuating, slowly evaporating world. Houses with shojis, sliding walls, which always created different spaces and shadows, with futons disappearing during the day, with bathrooms detached from the house, a place where the garden light flickers through rice paper walls. Faithful to the idea of the beautiful from the wabi-sabi tradition, derived from Zen, Tanizaki sang its praises.

Wabi: solitude, simplicity, melancholy, nature, sadness, asymmetry.
Sabi: the changing of time, the aging of objects, the patina of existence.

Tanizaki, the ironic, the refined and wise aesthete, who in the autumn of his life expressed his bizarre wish to have his daughter-in-law's footprints on his grave.

"So she can hear his bones crack, and even listen to him laugh."

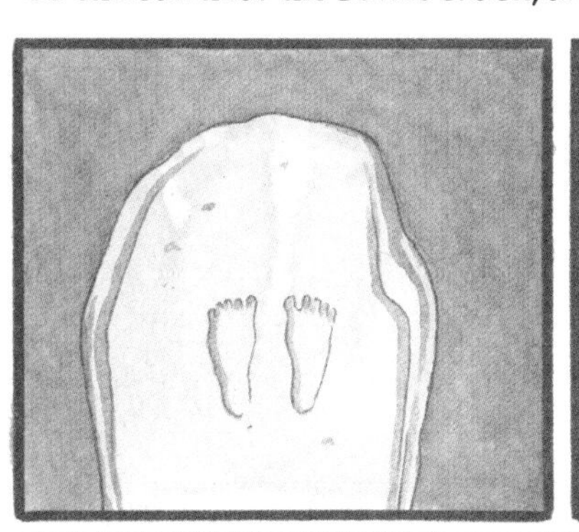

Pleasure and fetishistic worship, giving in to the brutal attraction to being subjugated by the beloved's desires, and finally become slave to them.

For years, his work, deemed offensive to public morality, was published with fuseji, a practice that substituted "forbidden" words with an x or a circle. Stirring up the reader's imagination, perhaps far beyond the author's. In the '50s, mores having changed, Tanizaki was asked to replace the fuseji with the original words, a proposal at which he smirked and replied:

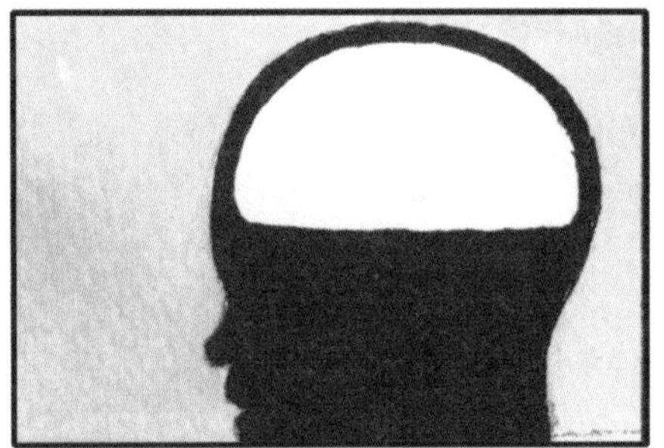

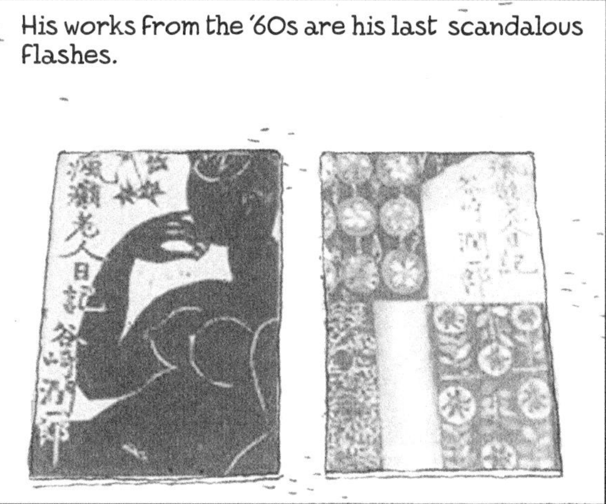

1962, "Diary of a Mad Old Man," in part autobiographical, recounts the attraction of the elderly Tokusuke to his own daughter-in-law. Satsuko, with stealthy beauty and libertine habits (she has a lover, watches boxing matches, wears Western clothes, drives a car), helps him to face his fear of death.

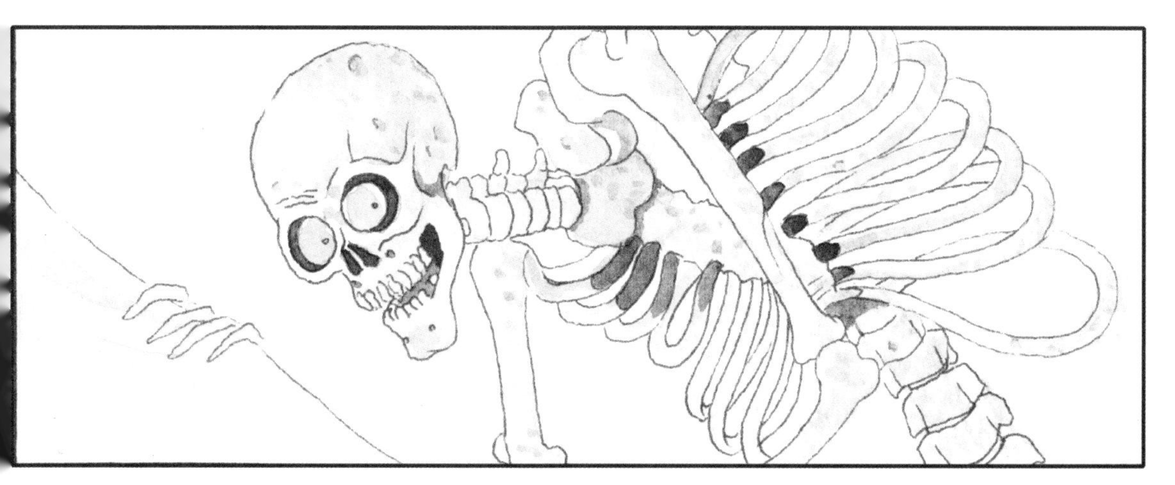

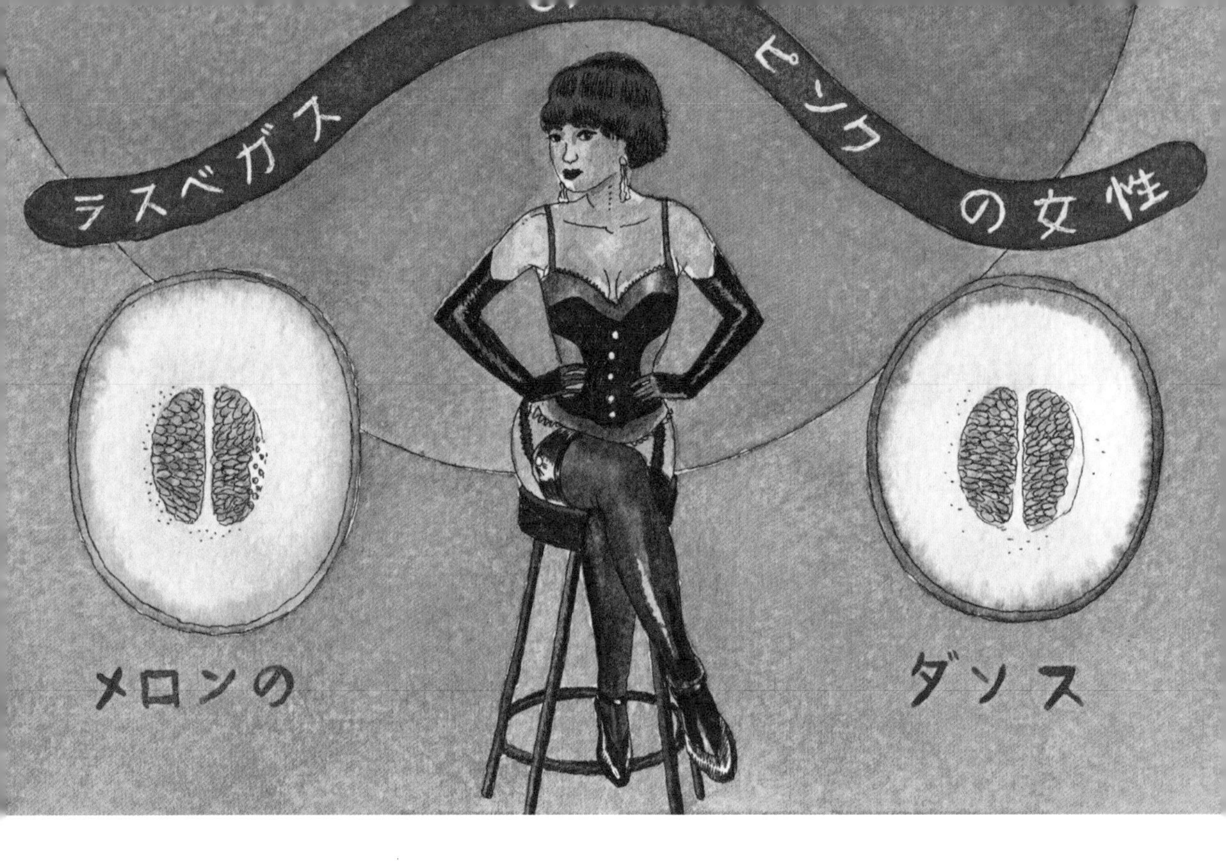

At the Tower Records store, where I would go every now and then to stock up on music, I found flyers for a nightspot in Akasaka Heights, a residential area of Tokyo. The locale was called The Deep, and it was no more than a fair-sized cellar in a modern building. At The Deep, the spot for the city's underground scene, they had theme nights. That night, I remember, was the "melon dance."

Every Wednesday, Tomoko danced with the Las Vegas Pink Ladies. She did it for herself, for fun. On other nights, she was a "water girl" at a club in Roppongi.
And she didn't like it.

The "water trade" is a centuries-old ritual (from the Tokugawa period) and indicates the practice of warm baths with more or less sexual massage. Today a water girl is halfway between hostess and geisha.

A 1956 law prohibits prostitution, but lends itself to various interpretations that have fostered the spread of mizu-shobai, the water trade. Thus many locales that advertise Turkish baths actually offer something else. In the Kabuchi-cho area, the excessive number of "Turkish baths" in the Shinjuku red light district led to an official objection from the government in Ankara, who found the image of the Turkish bath as a place of disrepute damaging.

Roppongi is the entertainment district, not as seedy as Kabuki-cho.

Tomoko receives salarymen looking for distraction. There are rules. The clients can touch her as they like, but can't "officially" go any further.

If they want, the clients organize a romantic candlelight dinner, a "dohan," where they play the part of the lady-killer and get the girl's telephone number. It's a dream for purchase, the rules are clear to everyone. Once the dinner is over, they go back to the club in Roppongi to drink. She's sick of that life. Tomoko is sick of seedy Love Hotels. But she's not desperate. She smiles. "I don't know what else I'd do."

The word "iki" comes from Ancient Chinese. In the Chinese pronunciation, sui, it means things worthy of great attention. In the Genroku period (1688–1704), the term appeared in erotic literature, indicating "someone who is very skilled in the arts of love and has a deep knowledge of human emotions."

Later, in the Bunka–Bunsei period (1804–1829), the word was used for the aesthetic of the places where prostitution was practiced, and therefore a certain style of typical geisha behavior.

Iki is composed of three stages: seduction, spiritual energy, and surrender.

Speaking to a man in a low voice, like a mezzo-soprano, is sensual without being cloying. You have to extend your words longer than necessary and then cut them off suddenly, emphasizing the intonation. This is seduction, this is iki.

Visually, iki is slightly inclined posture with a regal stride. Which, as opposed to the man's upright posture, signifies seduction and expresses the active movement toward the opposite sex and the passive movement of receiving him. Western-style seduction, which makes a show of itself, swaying blatantly, is as far as can be from the spirit of iki.

Iki is also the sight of a woman coming out of the bath. The seduction lies in the lingering awareness of her recent nakedness. Utamaro did not neglect to include a woman fresh out of water among the subjects of his female portraits.

I set off for the gardens of the Nezu Shrine, immersed in that silence that seemed frozen in time.

I thought of the cult of calm, devotedly cultivated throughout the centuries.

At the same time, the cult of war had blossomed.

History settles in places, like the dust of existence. Boom Boom Boom—I almost felt like I could hear the roar of the cannons, muffled by the silence of those gardens.

ada Abe, the muse of many artists and eccentrics, was born during one of the many twentieth-
entury wars.

ad been pondering telling her story for a long time. A life lost in pursuit of the ideals of beauty and
assion. Everyone knew her tragic ending in the West, thanks to Nagisa Oshima's film, "In the Realm of
e Senses" (Ai no korida).

ut I was interested less in the spectacular finale and more in her everyday life, composed of dreams and
rning disappointments. So far from convention, yet so hopelessly embroiled in the rules of iki. The
les of seduction, spiritual energy, and surrender.

at's it. If I had to think of a setting for Sada Abe's story, it would start like this: a warship in the Sea of
apan . . .

BOUM! BOUM!

BOUM

BDOUM

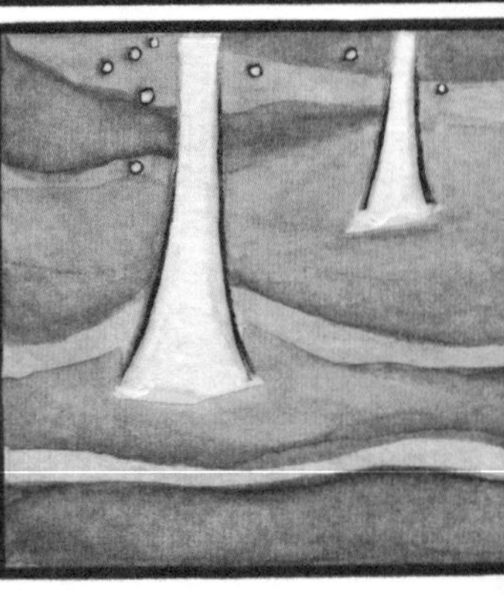

This is the battleship "Misaka" of Admiral Togo, who faced the Russian fleet in the Baltic in the Battle of Tsushima, between May 27 and 28, 1905.

That same night, the thirty-eighth year in the Meiji period, as the fleet of the Rising Sun destroys the Russian Imperial fleet—twice as big as theirs—the seventh daughter of Kingo Abe, a tatami merchant from Tokyo, is born.

Japan's control over Manchuria and Korea is assured. Long live the emperor!

In a house in Kanda-ku, in Tokyo, the first cries of Abe's daughter, who will be named Sada.

Seven years later, the death of the emperor. It is the end of an era, but the Abe family does not seem concerned. Little Sada dreams of becoming a famous geisha.

*shamisen: a traditional Japanese string instrument.

At nine, Sada is seen naked in a bath for men. A premonition of her turbulent life?

Then at the age of 14, raped by a student at the University of Keyo.

From that moment on, she starts hanging around with gangsters. Sada abandons her studies.

The whirlwind begins at just 15, when she sparks up romances with two men in their twenties.

Then her brother Kintaro runs away with the family money, leaving the Abes in a condition of sudden indigence. So they move to Saitama Kan, where she has other flirtations, other relationships.

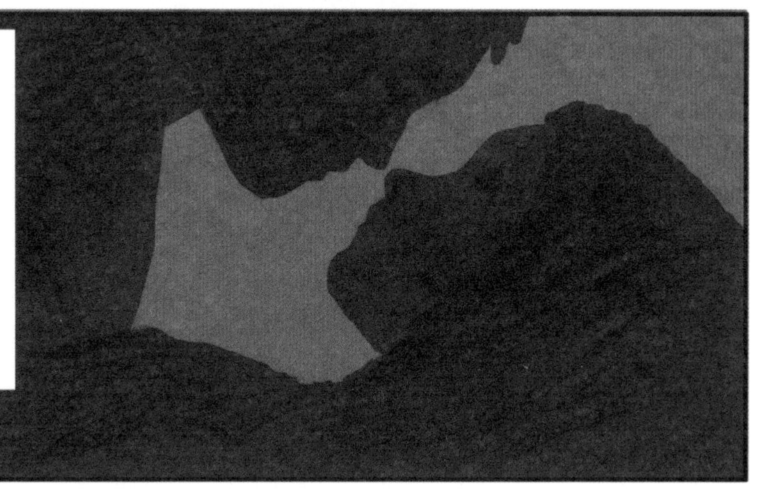

Then, at her insistence, she is taken to Yokohama, where she is sold to the geisha house of Inaba Masatake. Sada is 15.
Here we are, my girl.

Hmpf . . . she's a little advanced in age. We are a house of class. We'll see what we can do, Abe San.

A long apprenticeship begins. Then the man, judging her already "lost," takes advantage of her.
Now what, Inaba San?
Within a year, Sada is deemed ready, and she enters in the circle of geishas in Harijinmino, near Yokohama.

But not having started as a young girl, she remains a "maiko," an apprentice of the lowest rank.

Thus she is relegated to base and humiliating tasks, like sexually satisfying the customers of the geishas themselves.

The following year, 1923, Sada dreams of moving to a different area.

A terrible earthquake, magnitude 7.9, strikes the Kanto plain, on Japan's largest island. It is the morning of September 1, 1923. Since it happens at a time of day when people are cooking, several fires break out, destroying entire neighborhoods of the city.

Her life: a vortex of events, places, and lovers, that leads her to understand one thing clearly; she has a voracious appetite for sex. Frightened, she asks the doctors for comfort. "All normal," was the diagnosis. Then death suddenly strikes her mother.

A short time passes and the parade of lovers return, incessant.

Until, one day, in Nagoya . . .

Goro Omiya is a professor running for the elections for the Japan National Diet (Kokkai), the legislative body. Sada finds him a willing ear, so she pretends to be a widow and mother of a nine-year-old daughter, forced to work to support her. Feeling sorry for her, he gives her money and they become lovers.

Then another escape, this time from Nagoya to Tokyo, back to Inaba San.

She takes up prostitution again. Omiya tries to dissuade her, in vain.

A year later, her father dies, and she begins working as a waitress at the restaurant Yoshidaya. She is about to have the encounter that will change her life forever.

He, Kichizo Ishida, is the owner of that restaurant.

The two started up a secret relationship. One day when the geisha isn't there, they make love in her room.

Thereafter, it's a wild race to find a spot to steal away together: the hotel Mitsuwa, where their relationship turns pathological, excessive. Then they go to the hotel Tagawa. One day, Sada goes running to Omiya to ask for money, and then back to Ishida.
The couple has a mock wedding with the geishas.

A race to the bottom. Constant lack of funds. Sleep, reduced to the minimum, spaces out their long lovemaking sessions. Cutting their pubic hair, increasing excesses, lead to a bloody bite on Kichi's penis. Then they begin the practice of strangulation. Kichi is the one to teach Sada, and the pleasure becomes more and more intense.

More lies, this is Goro Omiya's lot. Sada brazenly lies to her benefactor.

She must absolutely find the means to continue her journey into the vortex of the senses.

Just before that, he goes back to his wife for three days, and she to Inaba.

The absence seemed endless, unbearable. To pass the time, Sada goes to Meiji-za to see a play at the theater. The story is about a woman who kills her lover. Inspired, Sada sells her kimono to buy a knife.

After strangling him to death, she castrates her beloved. With his blood, she writes on the body, "Sada and Kichi, only us two." Then she goes wandering around with his penis wrapped up in a bag.

This is the story of Sada Abe, who was sentenced to six years' imprisonment, even though she wanted the death penalty. Her lover's consent in the erotic game was considered fundamental. Against her wishes, on May 17, 1941, Sada was released for good behavior. She had become a celebrity all over Japan.

I experience the present in Japan as if there is a thin veil that lets the past shine through.

When I see an old postcard with this red tower for the first time, I feel like I'm traveling back in time.

This was the first Japanese skyscraper. It was erected in the Asakusa district in the late 1800s.

They called it Ryounkaku, the pavilion that goes beyond the clouds.

Once a disreputable area with many theaters (including the Denki-Kan, the first "electric" theater, which was already a cinema in 1903) and pleasure houses.

About Asakusa and its people, Yasunari Kawabata wrote: "They have a sense of duty all their own . . . and the thugs in Shibuya and Shinjuku are a new species. They have no tradition. The people from Asakusa do."

The modernist wonder was erected in that neighborhood in 1890, the twelve-story red tower, 225 feet tall.

From the ninth and tenth floors, you could admire the panorama, all of Tokyo as far as the eye could see, and on clear days you could even get a glimpse of Mt. Fuji.

It wasn't only a commercial building, since it also hosted cultural events: concerts, including Western music, geisha photo exhibits, beauty contests.

People came from all over Japan to see the sight. This marvel, however, had a short life, as it was destroyed in the terrible tremors of the Great Kanto Earthquake in 1923.

The Asakusa district, as well as two-thirds of the city of Tokyo, was devastated by the fire that razed it to the ground.

In that area, inhabited by artisans, many of whom were leather workers, lived the so-called "burakumin," people whose profession had to do with blood, activities considered to be degrading.

Mikiko says that the question of burakumin is very delicate, not so much in Tokyo as in Kyoto and Osaka, where burakumin were made to live in ghettos.

I realize the gravity of the implications when she tells me that every Japanese company has access to a database of names of burakumin families and that they avoid hiring the descendants of members of that untouchable caste.

This is a subject that people are hesitant to talk about, perhaps because it reveals the ancient roots of a racism that has endured through the centuries.

The origins of this discrimination lie in the Shinto tradition, which has an aversion to tasks that are considered impure, such as tanning hide or butchering animals. Seems like something from the past, and yet . . .

In Japan, like in ancient India, there were four castes: the samurai, farmers, artisans, and merchants.

The burakumin were beneath all of them, in every way considered degraded, untouchable. And this included not only people who had contact with blood for their trade (executioners, butchers, tanners, gravediggers) but also ex-convicts, beggars, prostitutes, street sweepers, acrobats, and other entertainers.

Historically, burakumin were isolated in separate neighborhoods. Anyone of humble origins could fall into that category if found guilty of certain impure acts, such as incest, or worse, bestiality.

This is why they were called "hinin," non-human, or "eta," literally abundance of filth. Moreover, if say a farmer's daughter, a member of a higher class, was driven to prostitution due to economic difficulties, then her origins were irrelevant and she would have been considered to all effects and purposes a burakumin.

On the other side, it was impossible for burakumin to move up to a higher class.

Burakumin was a mark of disgrace that extended to subsequent generations, guilty of nothing but descending from that particular family.

I look back at photos from long ago, and an old Kurosawa film comes to mind, "The Lower Depths" (Donzoko) set in the Tokyo underworld. Released in 1957, it depicts the life of the rejects in the ghettoes.

During the Meiji period—the mid 1800s—castes were abolished, and the so-called "degraded" were considered "new citizens" (a cunning way of distinguishing them nonetheless from old citizens, members of the higher classes). Regardless, the old citizens declared their disgust at being officially made the same as the untouchables, and they coined the term "burakumin," apparently less pejorative than "non-human" or "filth."

In 2014, I was in Tokyo when, during the course of some research, I came across some maps. They were centuries old, and marked the ghetto quarters of old Edo (now Tokyo) and Osaka, which I had talked about a few days before with Mikiko.

A scandal erupted because Google Maps superimposed the old maps with the city photographed by satellite, effectively revealing the areas where the untouchables and their descendants lived. The Japanese government demanded an official apology. These maps were deleted from the site a few days later.

It's clear that the free circulation of information reopens a wound that had never really healed in the Land of the Rising Sun, given that three million burakumin descendants would prefer that this sad story of discrimination and segregation be finally forgotten.

"Today there are agencies that provide us with data, entire family trees, family records, etc., and when we believe that someone is a descendent of burakumin we investigate further. If the results confirm it, we avoid hiring that person."

So declares a hiring manager at a large Japanese company, speaking on the condition of guaranteed anonymity for herself and her company.

The Japanese government issued a statement blaming Google Maps. And Google Maps obviously claims to be in favor of human rights but speaks in terms of historical interest.

They are two faces of the same hypocrisy, since neither does anything to help end this discrimination.

In my periodic comings-and-goings, my collaboration with Tsutsumi San intensified. Over the years, he continually raised the bar, getting more and more specific.

"I want all the dialogue to sound normal. You write 'Sure, it wouldn't be so bad to live underwater all the time. If not for . . .' Who is the character talking to? Isn't it ridiculous for him to talk to himself?"
Or:
"Igoruto San, you should consider this approach: one balloon per panel. Avoid balloons with too much text. Of course there may be exceptions, but for ease of reading it's important for everything to be completely clear."

We wanted to be able to communicate with readers as well as possible, and although I was clearly perceived as an alien author within the manga tradition, everyone—Tsutsumi, Kurihara—I, had the impression that a bridge was possible.

すぐ目に飛び込む
朱色がなんだか
とてもワクワクさせて
くれます。3才の息子と
ユーリの世界で遊んで
みたいです！
なんという不思議な絵
でしょう。とても心が和
やかになる様な絵です。
カラーなので1枚1枚切
り取って、額に入れています。
ユーリグッズができたら
いいですね。
セル画だったら少々高くても
買いたいくらいです。
843-03
佐賀県藤津郡嬉野町
下野甲1080-9
井口和文 ・25歳
会社員 ・0954-43-1626

Postcards and letters kept coming from readers. Obviously there were also some disapproving messages, but most of the fans seemed involved.

"First of all, Yuri is so cute and his stories are simple and original. I don't have any children, why don't you make a Yuri doll?"

(Professional, 34)

"I would like to ask you to make a book. I teach at an elementary school and I'd like to try to translate it into English for my students. The drawings are so good that I think they would be engaged."

(Schoolteacher, 29)

"Yuri is cute, maybe because of the colors, he gives me a sense of nostalgia."

(Housewife, 28)

"I like Yuri's face, you should make products as soon as possible. I'm waiting."

(Housewife, 39)

"I'm crazy about Yuri's world, it's so mysterious. Please put out merchandise."

(Freelancer, 37)

"Yuri, increase the number of panels or pages."

(Student, 21)

Encouraged by these messages, Mr. Udagawa had started developing a product line to help Yuri grow in readers' hearts. They made alarm clocks, eating utensils, kids' placemats, silk scarves, even phone cards, sweatshirts, backpacks, coin purses.
It was an explosion of "kawaii," or cuteness, as we would say. A childlike, comforting way of seeing the world.
A philosophical category, which obviously concealed its dangers.
During wartime, it was used to make everything seem cute, and the involvement of children not just acceptable, but right.
The "kawaii" narrative of the war was an unexpected discovery, which happened one day in 1996.

Would you like to draw eight color pages of Brillo, the little soldier? In Japan there were mangas about dumb yet cheerful soldiers called Norakuro and Robot Santohei. There are no cute stories about soldiers around now.

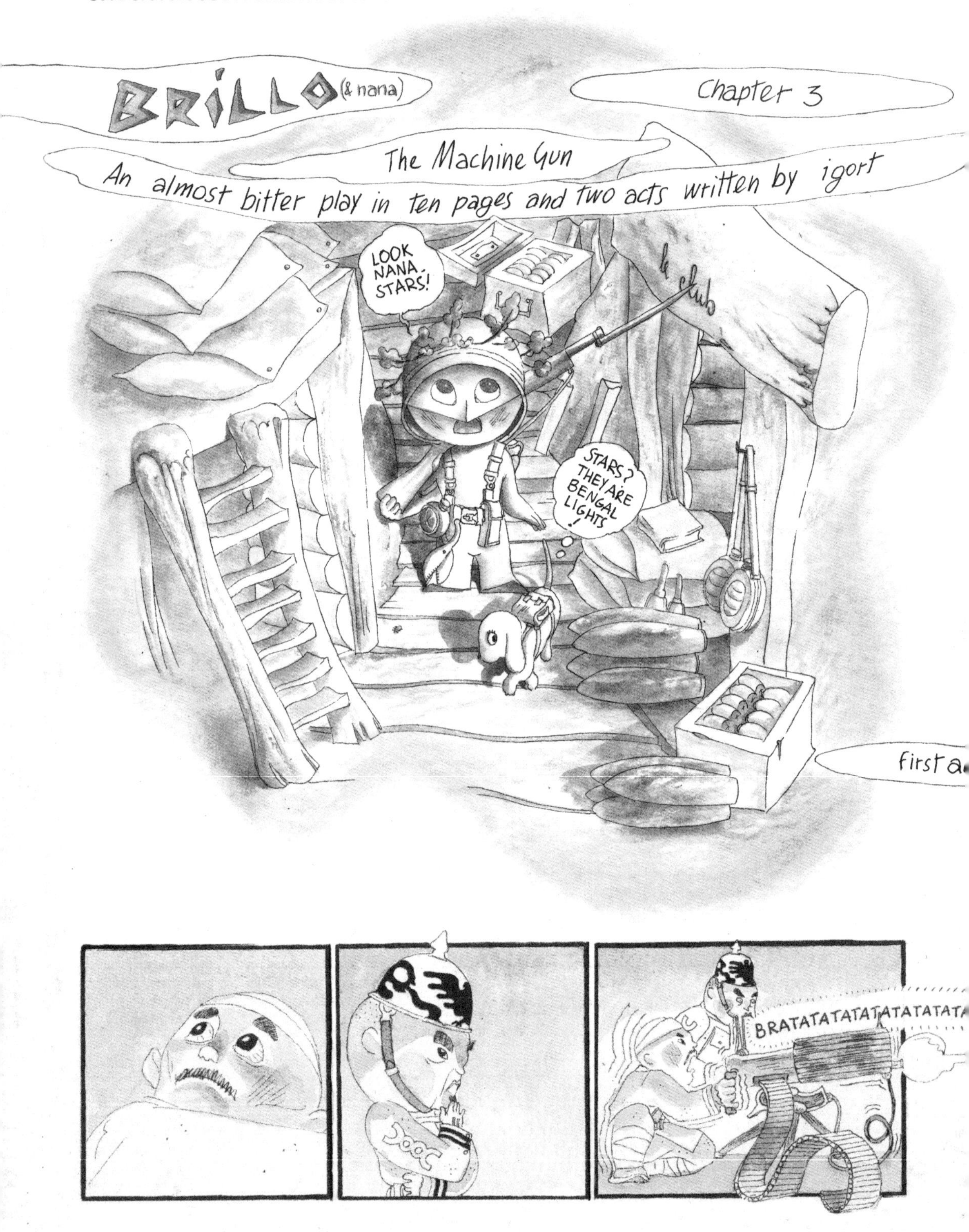

On the steps of a store in Shibuya, I noticed a discounted videotape of an animated film called "Momotaro–Umi no Shinpei." I had no clue what it was, but the images on the box were great.

I soon discovered that it was an animated war propaganda movie made by thirty-four-year-old socialist Mitsuyo Seo. I bought it unopened, and when I got around to watching it I was blown away by the grace and sublime beauty of the animation. Seo was clearly a giant.

Those warrior bunnies, monkeys, bears, and pheasants didn't just tell stories about battles and victory.

Rather, they showed the ending of a happy time. The four little animals and a little boy said goodbye to their families—Japan had entered the war. Goodbye to the paradise on the shores of the Pacific.

It was the twilight, described in a few, spare, perfect signs.

Needless to say, many themes of later Nipponese narrative are indebted to this gem, which brought Osamu Tezuka, sixteen at the time, to tears.

The film was confiscated and burned by American troops during the occupation.

Now it has been revived thanks to a negative miraculously rediscovered in Shochiku Ofuna warehouses in 1983.

In the Jimbocho neighborhood I found my portal to another time—a multi-story bookstore with notebooks, books, magazines from every period. In that place, no one really knows why, people speak in a whisper. "It's a temple, a place of worship from a distant time," I told myself.

I found "Norakuro."

Its author: Suiho Tagawa. He was a mangaka with a weathered face; he resembled a Japanese print.

Norakuro was so popular that his publications, which halted during the war, upon popular demand came back after the conflict.

Even Osamu Tezuka, future father of "Astroboy," loved that playful comic and considered it one of his biggest influences.

There are 10 volumes of "Norakuro," high-quality publications, bound in paper and cloth, each packaged in a cloth sleeve, a little treasury published by Kodansha.

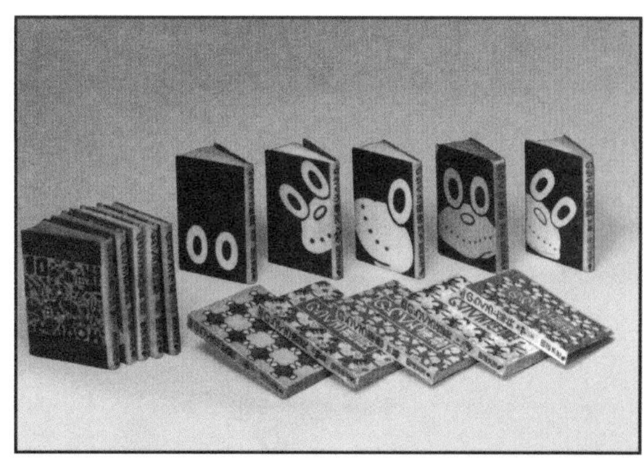

Tokyo Kanda—that was the name of the bookstore—is an unassuming building that reminds me of the used comics shops I would go to as a kid, when, immersed in paper dreams, I learned the magic power of books. Paper in Japan is an important thing. I linger for a while to look at the editions of Osamu Tezuka or Sampei Shirato with their rapturous colors . . .

. . . then I pick up two little volumes by Suiho Tagawa, open them, and the magic begins.

I am captivated not just by the smell of nearly a century that gives the paper the power to evoke the millions of events that the book has surely witnessed . . .

. . . but also the bright colors that the sepia patina of age has made so stirring. My heart leaps, I turn page after page trying to savor everything I see as much as I can.

And I see so much of Japan inside. I see a very young Suiho Tagawa, submitting the original pages of his manga to Kodansha in the '30s . . .

. . . in that little building that I myself have visited, with its imposing marble columns, its high-ceilinged rooms.

CLACK CLACK. I hear the sound of the geta and heels. I see the ritual bowing before every interaction, the cups of steaming green tea, the lit cigarettes in merchandising meetings, which in the case of the a young genius Tagawa were frequent, with an output comparable to what was produced for Disney in that period.

There were wooden items, metal toys, clocks, all with the faces and bodies of the characters brought to life, animated, not wanting to live on paper alone.

Yet here, in Japan, paper is shared territory. It bridges existence, a tactile existence, where roughness, wrinkles, transparency, semi-transparency, are important qualities.

Paper encloses objects, in the wrapping custom that places the sheets diagonally and not orthogonally (at right angles, as we do). Box tops, often made of lined cardboard, are printed with pressed ideograms, tone on tone, seemingly invisible. The wrapping paper around them creates other transparencies. Touch and sight, the play of seeing and not seeing become an art, a ritual, that reaches the sublime. Following a custom that celebrates "giving" as a symbolic act of sharing that's more important than the gift itself.

Paper also encloses the body, in a certain sense, since it is the material that the diaphanous, self-propelled screens called shoji are made of. It is a grounded life, that of the '30s. Japan hasn't yet been too contaminated by the West with its concept of the elevated seat. A bed isn't called a "beddo," it's a "futon," and it is tucked away in the closet once the light of day floods these houses of wood and rice paper.

Tokyo, capital of an enlightened democracy, is still a frozen city, which left its medieval past in the 1910s to transform into the capital of imperialist Japan of the Showa period. The new era which would see Hirohito come to power in 1926.

Tagawa sees the new path, and his dog character, Norakuro, is a soldier.

The young author had just finished service—a good three years in the army—as was the practice at the time. He satirizes this in his comic stories, transposes memories. So the dog goes to war.

(image from NORAKURO. Published by Kodansha, 1933)

And here is the tragic fate that makes these stories so moving, the fact that, as for the film "Momotaro" (from just a few years later) . . .

. . . the space of childhood is sullied, violated in its purity, by the idea of death and combat.

There is something desperately tragic and essentially Japanese in all this. A bitter smile brushed by a chrysanthemum.

On the shelves of my comics shop in Shibuya I also discovered "Grave of the Fireflies," a film that shook me up more than any other from those May days.

From a few years prior—1988—the same year as "My Neighbor Totoro," "Grave of the Fireflies" countered Miyazaki's charmed lightness with a haunting recollection of wartime Japan.

Isao Takahata, a friend and longtime collaborator of Miyazaki's, represented childhood with the same poetry, but seemed determined to climb a forbidden mountain: the idea that animated cartoons could be real dramas.

I don't know if Takahata was the first to harbor such an idea, but it didn't really matter. The cover of the video spoke volumes—this wasn't a cartoon for kids.

I paid and headed for the subway. I took the Ginza line toward home, impatient to change at Omotesando to the Chiyoda line. My imagination wandered, trying to picture what I was going to see.

I was sure I wouldn't be disappointed, and I was right. When the video began to play in my tape player, astonishment slowly gave way to admiration. And because of that sort of invisible magic that great works have, I began traveling in the film.

I entered the Tokyo of 50 years earlier to follow the story of Seita and Setsuko, two kids who were dealing with the struggles of a violent life in times of war. It was immediately clear that I was not seeing a consolatory film, because the story began with the end, with Seita's death. Takahata had taken a cue from the great anti-military cinema.

He followed the inspiration of his visionary talent and narrated in broad strokes. Characters defined with memorable scenes, a subdued sensibility and no indulgences. Takahata, it was clear, praised the human being, the little everyday things, only he did so with a new gaze, penetrating and engaged.

He made me think of the words of my editor, Tsutsumi San.

Setsuko and Seita lived in a world whose rules they neither understood nor accepted. A world that no longer considered innocence, and spoke the language of destruction.

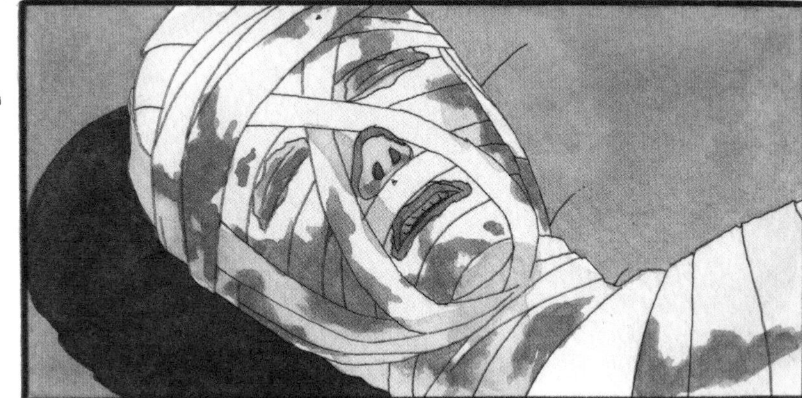

It was defeat. Human faltering at its own violence.

I never met Takahata, not even when I went to Studio Ghibli to meet Hayao Miyazaki. That day, despite all my preparations, I arrived late. The train for Higashi-Koganei had been stopped for almost an hour—someone had committed suicide. I waited, like everyone else, straining to hear the regularly transmitted announcements on JR.

I expected to see a skyscraper, but instead the most important animation studio in the Rising Sun was a simple, two-story building.

Miyazaki was kind. He spoke with the calm tone of the thoughtful.

Then he took me to the second floor, where I was able to see the animators at work. Most of them worked old style, by hand. Computers were used for the more technical parts. We went up to his studio. It was an atmosphere of great concentration.

Then, seeing my journal, he said that he too used to draw in notebooks. "That's where I got the best ideas for my movies, in peace, at the drawing board with some colored pencils and watercolors." He laughed, every now and then his glasses fogged up.

I told him that they were travel journals, mostly for notes. I loved less refined paper. Then we went down to the café on the first floor of Studio Ghibli, to have a coffee before saying goodbye.

He told me about when he did the "Nausicaa" manga, it took him so much time and energy that he considered cinema a cakewalk by comparison. "Manga isn't for me." We smiled, and then I left him to his work. It was one of the most carefree and profound afternoons of my life.

Tsuge's and Tatsumi's stories were sad. Mizuki's grotesque.

Stories of malaise, raw and full of deep psychological pain that sparked a movement on the pages of the underground magazine "GARO" in the '60s. The movement took the name "geki-ga" ("dramatic pictures") in contrast to the term "man-ga" (whimsical pictures").

The term "geki-ga" was coined in 1956 by Yoshihiro Tatsumi.

Japan, immediately after the war. A man stung by a jellyfish is losing blood from an artery and wandering through a fishing village on the Pacific asking for help, until he realizes that no one really cares about helping him—they're just waiting for him to die.

This is the plot of "Neji-shiki," Yoshiharu Tsuge's visionary masterpiece, which was also made into a film. Tsuge was the pioneer of a certain brand of story that was both gritty and poetic.

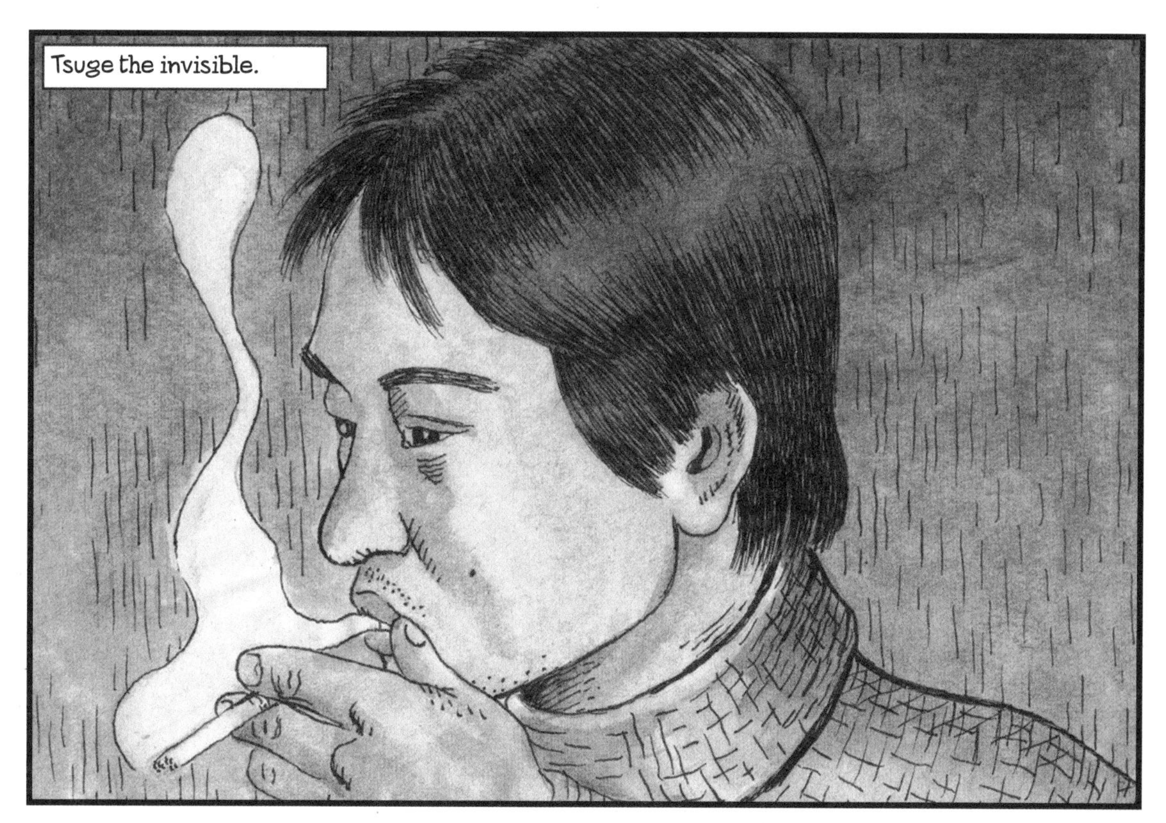

His stories were a hit
then he quit, suddenly,

and disappeared.

Immersed in his silent world, he refused visits and job offers. Even to be published abroad. Rumors spread: "he moved away from Tokyo;" "he left everything to become a hermit in the mountains." "No, he's sick." All theories that suggested isolation. Like the stories he had told so well.

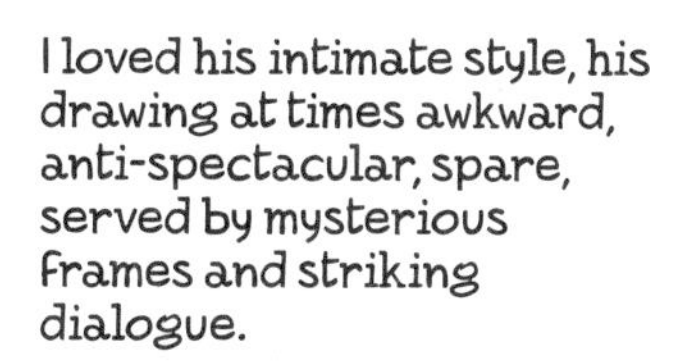

This comes from "The Man without Talent," a merciless account of the tribulations of a mangaka who takes any sort of work, trying to survive. Stories about losers, full of mystery and violence.

I had tried to meet Tsuge. Mikiko, after a little investigating, had found his number and called him on the phone. He was a solitary man, seemingly shy. I quickly realized that nothing was going to come of it.

Later on in our travels and get-togethers, I would spend hours talking about his work with Spiegelman or Mazzucchelli, who loved him as much as me.

Until one day, the latter, very excited, wrote me from Japan saying that he had met him. They talked about American comics from the '40s.

And Tsuge the invisible, interested in the comics of his childhood, had become a little less of a ghost again; he was human, after all. Consumed by shyness, but fundamentally someone who, like the rest of us, was crazy about drawing.

Born in 1922, he had a wretched life. In the Japanese army, during World War II, he contracted malaria and lost his left arm in an explosion.

In 1959 he published the volume "Kitaro of the Graveyard" ("Ge Ge Ge no Kitaro"), a dark, funny story, and it was clear to everyone that a star had been born. The nine-volume series had the honor, a few years later, of being adapted into an animated series, directed by Isao Takahata (with a full 65 episodes).

In his volumes, Mizuki, a skilled graphic alchemist, never ceased to surprise me. Capable as he was of joining the noble style of ukiyo-e with manga, of fusing the rigorous descriptive detail of Klinger or Doré with lines out of juvenile jokes, he never lost sight of the atmospheres he wanted to evoke.

The Japanese believe in the invisible, and to everyone it was abundantly clear that the stories of this master were a portal that opened up into the hidden part of the universe.

Kurihara San, head of the Seventh editorial division of Kodansha, told me one day that Japan was like a sealed box, and anyone who wanted to get to know it needed to have the keys to the box in order to appreciate the treasures kept inside of it. I studied it for over 20 years and I continually return to this place of the soul. Yet its mystery is constantly renewed.

イゴルト
マンガ家

Matsuo Basho was born in 1644. The son of a country samurai, he seemed destined to a military career, but being more inclined toward poetry, he began to write. Since Japan hadn't had any wars for over 60 years, the samurai were not doing so well economically.

At any rate, his father, as was the custom of the time, left what little wealth he had to his first born. Basho, whose real name was Matsuo Munefusa, was the third born. Before becoming Basho (banana tree), he had gone through about twenty names, and just before choosing Basho he went by Tosei, which means green peach.

He was a great walker, poet, nature lover. He believed that the path of poetry should follow the rhythm of the seasons.

Since he owned no property and lived on charity or small donations from disciples, Basho wasn't afraid of bandits. But his faithful followers trembled at the thought of him going all over Japan without being wary of the ill-intentioned.

He wrote many poems. One devoted to the banana tree was called "Words on Transplanting Banana Trees." The plant had been given to him by his favorite pupil. Its leaves grew so much they shaded the small hut where Basho lived.

He became interested in Zen and started to practice for a while under Bukkyo before returning to his beloved banana tree. One story goes that, one day, the master and another monk came to visit him. Bukkyo asked:

This would later become a famous haiku, to which Basho added a first verse that went: "Old pond, a frog jumps in, water's sound."

He died at fifty, one day before the eleventh month of 1694.
Along with Buson and Issa, he is considered the greatest haiku poet of all time.

Come out, come crawling out
underneath the silkworm hut
the voice of a toad.

Irises blooming
from my feet
sandals laced in blue.

Taros sprouting
at the gate,
young creepers.

The great masters of ancient tradition taught me, like Ekiken, to consider the elements of my modest existence. They were travel companions. In Japan, I felt like I rediscovered myself, that archipelago spoke to the island of my soul. With a fisherman's simple words, someone born near the water.

With Mikiko in a Shinjuku bookstore I had found the volumes of Hokusai, the ones that he called "manga." Books of drawings with just lines, perfect traces, in search of the harmony of forms. I traveled through those pages.

Hokusai was an unrivaled master in the art of ukiyo-e, Japanese prints. One of the greats, known for the boldness of his designs, the power of his visions. He lived to be eighty-nine.

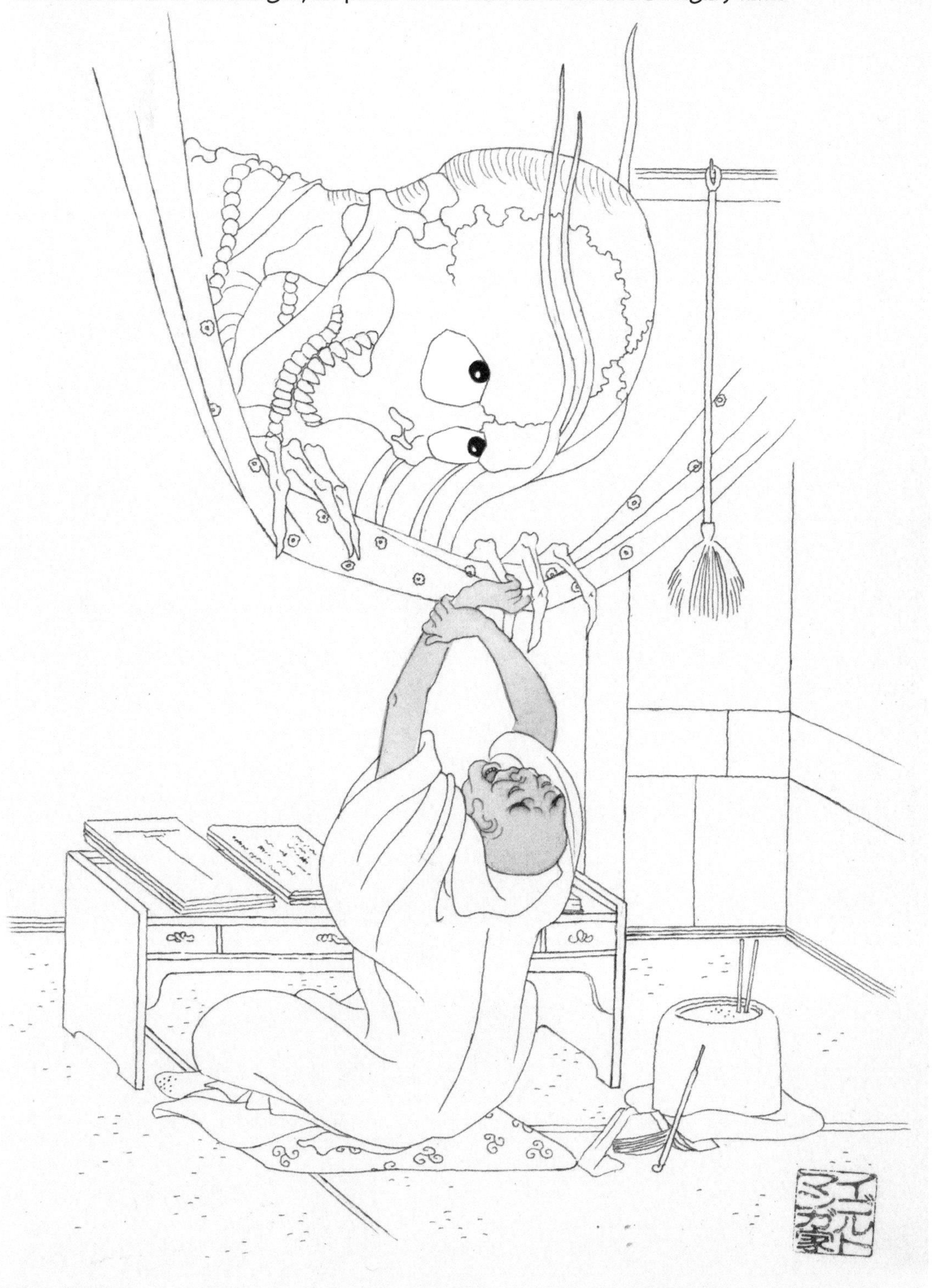

He had much glory and a legendary life. What is less well known is that the illustrious Hokusai was tormented by incompetent engravers.

These people, who traced his drawings and carved them onto blocks of wood, didn't stick to the original designs, but interpreted noses and ears as they wished, following the trends of the moment.

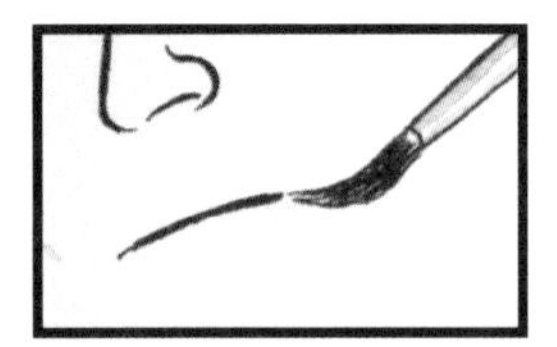

Hokusai was offended by this practice and incessantly wrote to them: "Carve the eyes without the lower eyelid. Please, I beg you. And make the noses after these two examples, and not like Utagawa."

The letter asking the publisher to talk to Hokusai's trusted engraver, Egawa, the only one the Master went to, was illustrated with examples. And it concluded with: "I implore you to devote a thought to this hopeless old man." A formula often used by beggars at the time.

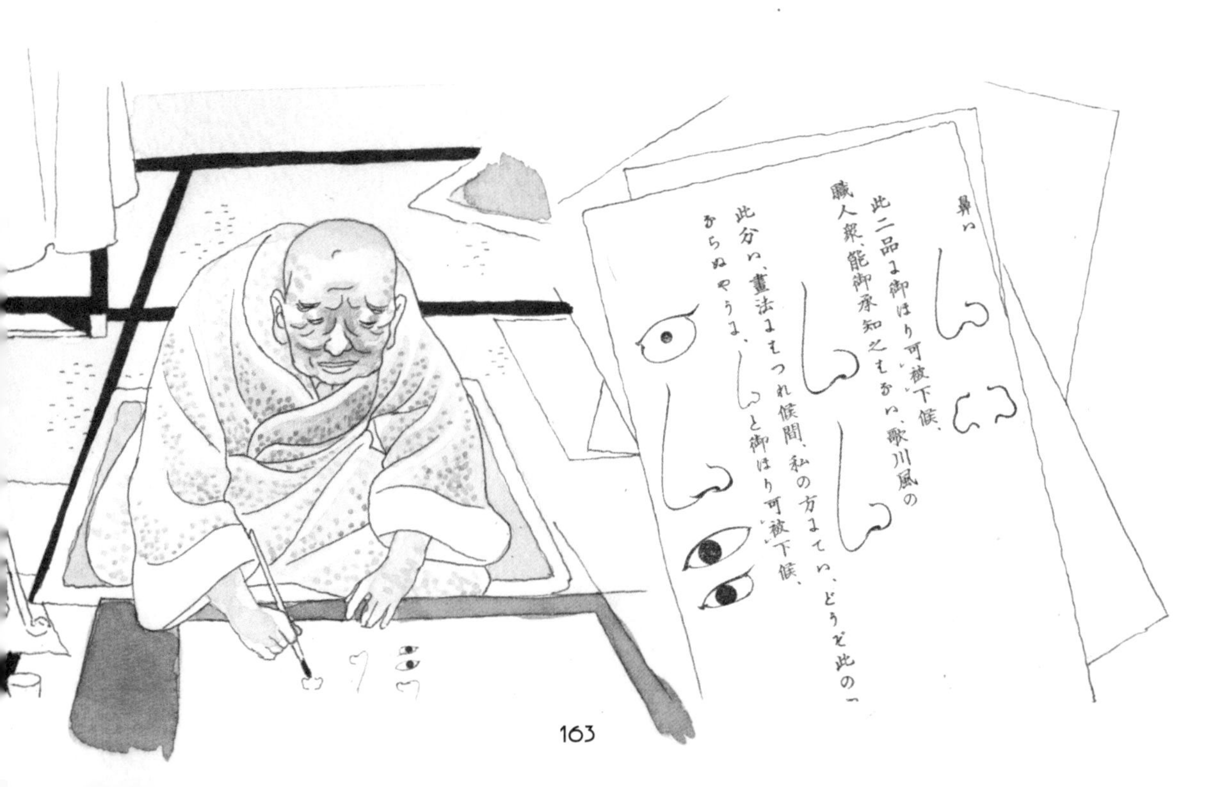

More than a century later, at the dawn of manga, the plates used to produce pages were still made by hand. The mangakas' drawings would be delivered to publishers who had artisans transfer them onto zinc plates. Those plates would become the stencils for the printing presses.

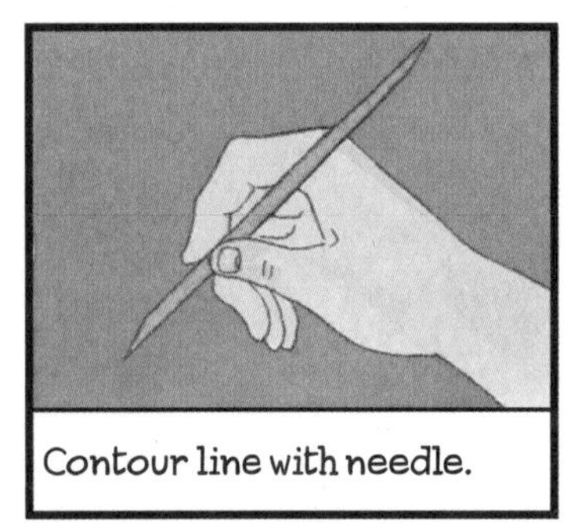

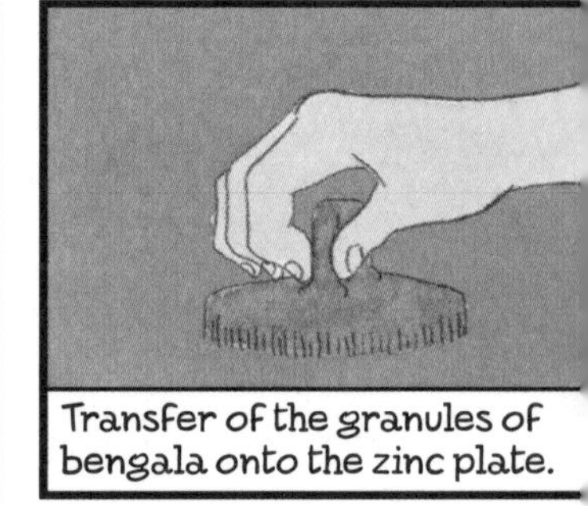

This technique was called "egakihan." In postwar Japan, this was the most common and economical method of reproduction.

Osamu Tezuka, as he writes in his manga autobiography, worked for publishers in Osaka, and one day gathered all his courage and asked:

reviously, before the new technology had made photographic reproduction of the original rawings possible, the young Tezuka did everything he could to convince the engravers not to alter is noses or ears according to changing trends or their own personal taste.

And although some time had passed, Tezuka, at the end of his career . . .

. admitted to suffering when seeing his work from a time demeaned by such an arbitrary technical tep. All this to say that great art, even when made with modesty, is often a matter of eyelids, noses, nd ears.

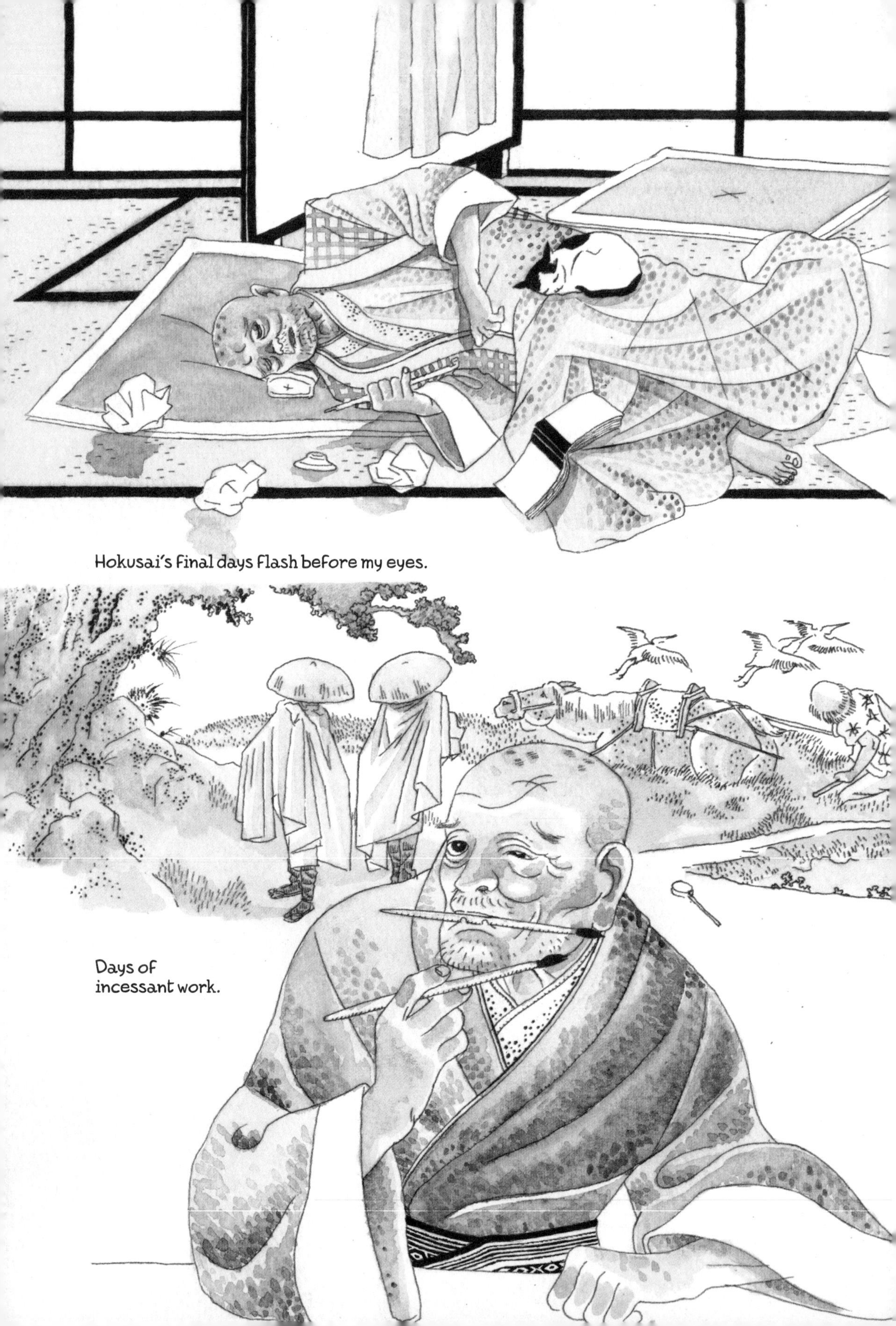
Hokusai's final days flash before my eyes.
Days of
incessant work.

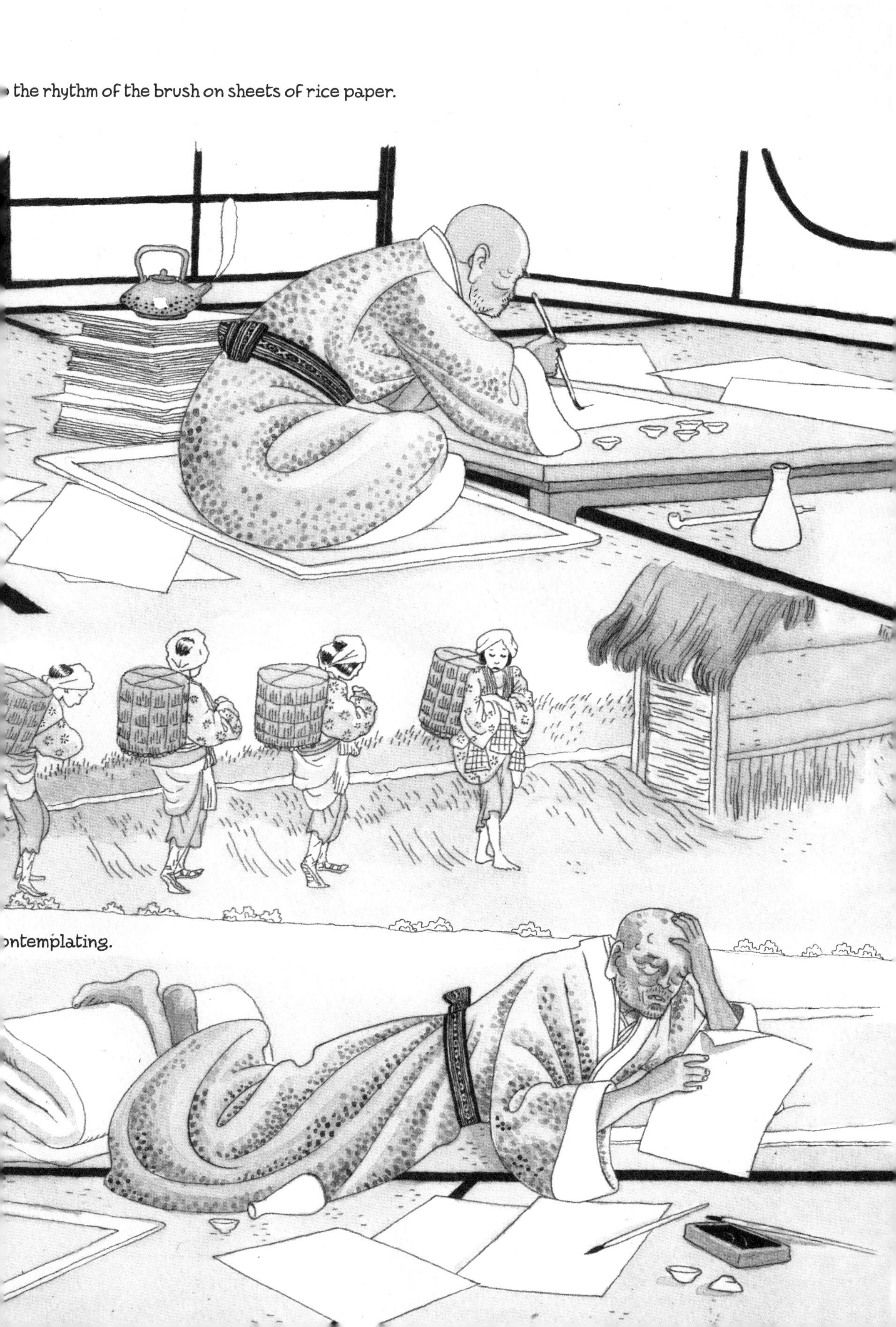
the rhythm of the brush on sheets of rice paper.
ontemplating.

This book is a time machine. It has allowed me to travel backwards for two years, east of myself. To rediscover the places, relive the emotions.

Thank you for having kept me company all this way, my reader friend.

The time to depart has come. Hokusai's last words:

"Since the age of six, I've had a mania for copying the forms of things,

among what I have depicted there is nothing worthy of consideration.

At seventy-three I have barely grasped the essence of the form of animals and birds, insects and fish, the life of herbs and plants.

At eighty-six I will progress further;

at ninety I will have worked out the hidden meaning even further,

and at one hundred perhaps I will have truly reached the dimension of the divine and marvelous.

When I am one hundred and ten, even just a dot or a line will be endowed with their own lives.

Declared by the old man crazy about painting."

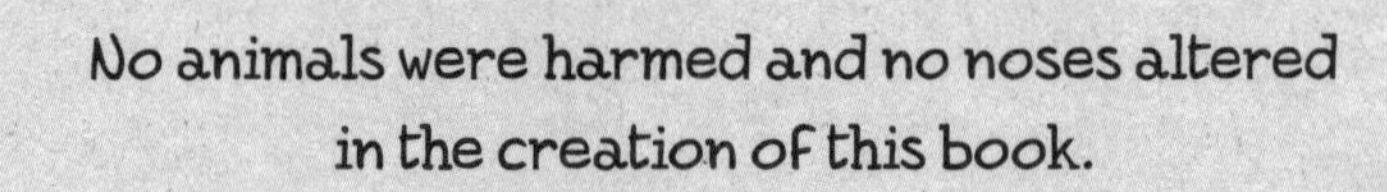

Dedicated to the memory of Katsushika Hokusai and Osamu Tezuka.

Igort. Tokyo, Paris, Capitana.

Igort
Miyazaki

Igort
Sakaguchi
Marzocchi
Jori

YURI
24 宇宙時間の色彩の冒険

月イチ連載
YURI
IGORT

はじめての冒険

YURI
IGORT

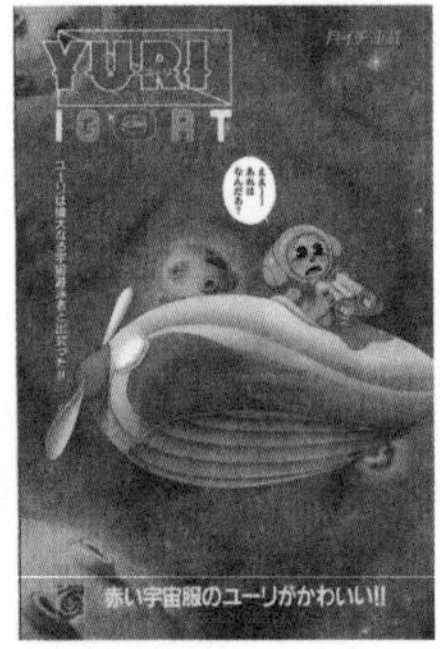
YURI
IGORT
赤い宇宙服のユーリがかわいい!!

YURI
IGORT
宇宙に浮かぶユーリがかわいい!!

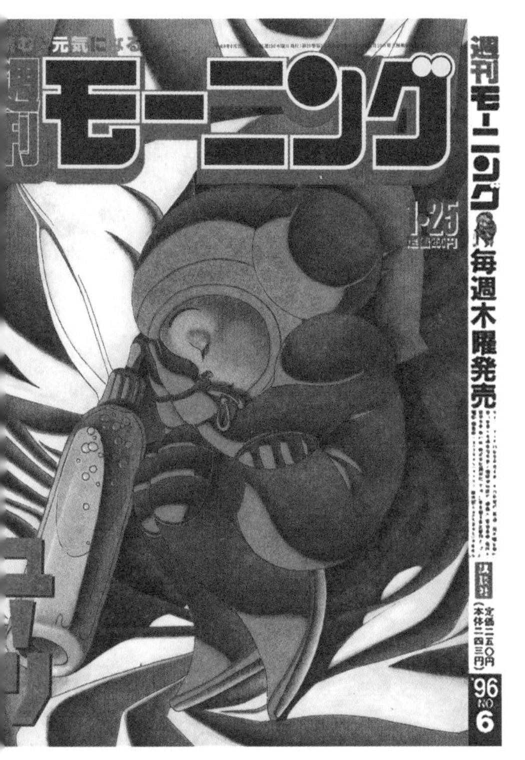

Kodansha Comic Morning redaction, 1996

Morning Magical Collection All c
YURI
[ユーリ]
「モーニング」連載中に
熱烈な応援の手紙を多数いただいた
小さなヒーロー、ユーリが
オールカラーの楽しい本になりました。
はじめての冒険
宇宙でいちばん小っちゃな宇宙飛行士ユーリの24宇宙時間の大きな
YURI
[ユーリ]
イゴルト
[ユーリ] IGORT[イゴルト]
7月23日(火)発売 定価/1300円
単行本のための本文書き下ろし12ページを含むオールカラー104

P.S. Midori's Dream

Just before putting this book to print I received a letter from Midori, my translator. "I saw it in a dream," she wrote. "I was in Kyoto, strolling through the old neighborhoods. It was the Meiji period, around the early 1900s."

In a fabric and kimono shop there was a high-class woman of a certain age, but with her back still erect. She had her white hair gathered up as they used to do, and she was absorbed in her tasks. I stared at her intently, and a voice in my mind said, "That lady is Igort."

I remember the dark, gleaming wood of that old store perfectly. The stone entrance. I stood there outside watching her for a long time. Her gestures were absolutely precise.
Her movements were calm.
The calm of someone who has lived a full life.

MY GRATITUDE TO

MIKIKO KIKUTA, COSTANTINO PRESS, DIMITRI MORETTI, ROBERTA NOVIELLI, GIORGIO AMITRANO, MIDORI YAMANE, GALYA SEMENIUK, LEILA MARZOCCHI, ANNALISA MONGILI, JACQUES DE LOUSTAL, DEBBIE BIBO, STEVE MOCKUS

FOR THEIR PRECIOUS SUPPORT AND HELP.

IGORT

FIRST PUBLISHED IN THE UNITED STATES IN 2017
BY CHRONICLE BOOKS LLC.

FIRST PUBLISHED IN ITALY IN 2015 BY COCONINO PRESS.

LIBRARY OF CONGRESS CATALOGING-IN-PUBLICATION
DATA IS AVAILABLE.

ISBN: 978-1-4521-5870-9

ARTWORK AND DESIGN BY IGORT

ENGLISH LANGUAGE TRANSLATION BY JAMIE RICHARDS

MANUFACTURED IN ITALY

10 9 8 7 6 5 4 3 2 1

CHRONICLE BOOKS LLC
680 SECOND STREET
SAN FRANCISCO, CA 94107
WWW.CHRONICLEBOOKS.COM